THE
Weapon
OF
Prayer

THE Weapon OF Prayer

E. M. BOUNDS

MOODY PRESS

CHICAGO

MOODY PRESS EDITION, 1980
ISBN 0-8024-6727-x

Printed in the United States of America

CONTENTS

I

PRAYER ESSENTIAL TO GOD

" Then shalt thou call, and the Lord shall answer; thou shalt cry, and he shall say, Here I am. 14th verse: Then shalt thou delight thyself in the Lord; and I will cause thee·to ride upon the high places of the earth, and feed thee with the heritage of Jacob thy father: for the mouth of the Lord hath spoken it."
— Isaiah 58: 9.

IT must never be forgotten that Almighty God rules this world. He is not an absentee God. His hand is ever on the throttle of human affairs. He is everywhere present in the concerns of time. "His eyes behold, his eyelids try the children of men." He rules the world just as He rules the Church by prayer. This lesson needs to be emphasized, iterated and reiterated in the ears of men of modern times and brought to bear with cumulative force on the consciences of this generation whose eyes have no vision for the eternal things, whose ears are deaf toward God.

Nothing is more important to God than prayer in dealing with mankind. But it is likewise all-important to man to pray. Failure to pray is failure along the whole line of life. It is failure of duty, service, and spiritual progress. God must help man by prayer. He who does not pray, therefore, robs himself of God's help and places God where He cannot help man. Man must pray to

9

God if love for God is to exist. Faith and hope, and patience and all the strong, beautiful, vital forces of piety are withered and dead in a prayerless life. The life of the individual believer, his personal salvation, and personal Christian graces have their being, bloom and fruitage in prayer.

All this and much more can be said as to the necessity of prayer to the being, and culture of piety in the individual. But prayer has a larger sphere, a more obligated duty, a loftier inspiration. Prayer concerns God, whose purposes and plans are conditioned on prayer. His will and His glory are bound up in praying. The days of God's splendour and renown have always been the great days of prayer. God's great movements in this world have been conditioned on, continued and fashioned by prayer. God has put Himself in these great movements just as men have prayed. Present, prevailing, conspicuous and mastering prayer has always brought God to be present. The real and obvious test of a genuine work of God is the prevalence of the spirit of prayer. God's mightiest forces surcharge and impregnate a movement when prayer's mightiest forces are there.

God's movement to bring Israel from Egyptian bondage had its inception in prayer. Thus early did God and the human race put the fact of prayer as one of the granite forces upon which His world movements were to be based.

Hannah's petition for a son began a great prayer movement for God in Israel. Praying women, whose prayers like those of Hannah, can give to the cause of God men like Samuel, do more for the Church and the world than all the politicians on earth. Men born of prayer are the saviours of the state, and men saturated with prayer give life and impetus to the Church. Under God they are saviours and helpers of both Church and state.

We must believe that the divine record of the facts about prayer and God are given in order that we might be constantly reminded of Him, and be ever refreshed by the faith that God holds His Church for the entire world, and that God's purpose will be fulfilled. His plans concerning the Church will most assuredly and inevitably be carried out. That record of God has been given without doubt that we may be deeply impressed that the prayers of God's saints are a great factor, a supreme factor, in carrying forward God's work, with facility and in time. When the Church is in the condition of prayer God's cause always flourishes and His kingdom on earth always triumphs. When the Church fails to pray, God's cause decays and evil of every kind prevails. In other words, God works through the prayers of His people, and when they fail Him at this point, decline and deadness ensue. It is according to the divine plans that spiritual prosperity comes through the prayer-channel. Praying saints are God's agents for carrying on His saving and providential work on earth. If His agents fail Him, neglecting to pray, then His work fails. Praying agents of the Most High are always forerunners of spiritual prosperity.

The men of the Church of all ages who have

held the Church for God have had in affluent fulness and richness the ministry of prayer. The rulers of the Church which the Scriptures reveal have had preëminence in prayer. Eminent, they may have been, in culture, in intellect and in all the natural or human forces; or they may have been lowly in physical attainments and native gifts; yet in each case prayer was the all potent force in the rulership of the Church. And this was so because God was with and in what they did, for prayer always carries us back to God. It recognizes God and brings God into the world to work and save and bless. The most efficient agents in disseminating the knowledge of God, in prosecuting His work upon the earth, and in standing as breakwater against the billows of evil, have been praying Church leaders. God depends upon them, employs them and blesses them.

Prayer cannot be retired as a secondary force in this world. To do so is to retire God from the movement. It is to make God secondary. The prayer ministry is an all-engaging force. It must be so, to be a force at all. Prayer is the sense of God's need and the call for God's help to supply that need. The estimate and place of prayer is the estimate and place of God. To give prayer the secondary place is to make God secondary in life's affairs. To substitute other forces for prayer, retires God and materializes the whole movement.

Prayer is an absolute necessity to the proper carrying on of God's work. God has made it so. This must have been the principal reason why in the early Church, when the complaint that the widows of certain believers had been neglected in the daily administration of the Church's benefactions, that the twelve called the disciples together, and told them to look out for seven men, " full of the Holy Ghost, and wisdom," who they would appoint over that benevolent work, adding this important statement, " But we will give ourselves continually to prayer and to the ministry of the Word." They surely realized that the success of the Word and the progress of the Church were dependent in a preëminent sense upon their " giving themselves to prayer." God could effectively work through them in proportion as they gave themselves fully to prayer.

The Apostles were as dependent upon prayer as other folks. Sacred work,—Church activities— may so engage and absorb us as to hinder praying, and when this is the case, evil results always follow. It is better to let the work go by default than to let the praying go by neglect. Whatever affects the intensity of our praying affects the value of our work. " Too busy to pray " is not only the keynote to backsliding, but it mars even the work done. Nothing is well done without prayer for the simple reason that it leaves God out of the account. It is so easy to be seduced by the good to the neglect of the best, until both the good and the best perish. How easily may men, even leaders in Zion, be led by the insidious wiles of Satan to cut short our praying in the interests of the work! How easy to neglect prayer or abbreviate our praying simply by the plea that we have Church work on our hands. Satan has effectively disarmed us when he can keep us too busy doing things to stop and pray.

"Give ourselves continually to prayer and the ministry of the word." The Revised Version has it, "We will continue steadfastly in prayer." The implication of the word used here means to be strong, steadfast, to be devoted to, to keep at it with constant care, to make a business out of it. We find the same word in Colossians 4: 12, and in Romans 12: 12, which is translated, "Continuing instant in prayer."

The Apostles were under the law of prayer, which law recognizes God as God, and depends upon Him to do for them what He would not do without prayer. They were under the necessity of prayer, just as all believers are, in every age and in every clime. They had to be devoted to prayer in order to make their ministry of the Word efficient. The business of preaching is worth very little without it be in direct partnership with the business of praying. Apostolic preaching cannot be carried on unless there be apostolic praying. Alas, that this plain truth has been so easily forgotten by those who minister in holy things! Without in any way passing a criticism on the ministry, we feel it to be high time that somebody or other declared to its members that effective preaching is conditioned on effective praying. The preaching which is most successful is that ministry which has much of prayer in it. Perhaps one might go so far as to say that it is the only kind that *is* successful. God can mightily use the preacher who prays. He is God's chosen messenger for good, whom the Holy Spirit delights to honour, God's efficient agent in saving men and in edifying the saints.

In Acts 6: 1–8 we have the record of how, long ago, the Apostles felt that they were losing—had lost—in apostolic power because they did not have relief from certain duties in order that they might give themselves more to prayer. So they called a halt because they discovered to their regret that they were too deficient in praying. Doubtless they kept up the form of praying, but it was seriously defective in intensity and in point of the amount of time given to it. Their minds were too much preoccupied with the finances of the Church. Just as in this day we find in many places both laymen and ministers are so busily engaged in " serving tables," that they are glaringly deficient in praying. In fact in present-day Church affairs men are looked upon as religious because they give largely of their money to the Church, and men are chosen for official positions not because they are men of prayer, but because they have the financial ability to run Church finances and to get money for the Church.

Now these Apostles, when they looked into this matter, determined to put aside these hindrances growing out of Church finances, and resolved to " give themselves to prayer." Not that these finances were to be ignored or set aside, but ordi-

nary laymen, " full of faith and the Holy Ghost "
could be found, really religious men, who could
easily attend to this money business without in the
least affecting their piety or their praying, thus
giving them something to do in the Church, and at
the same time taking the burden from the Apostles
who would be able now to pray more, and praying
more, to be blessed themselves in soul, and at the
same time to more effectually do the work to which
they had been called.

They realized, too, as they had not realized before, that they were being so pressed by attention
to material things, things right in themselves, that
they could not give to prayer that strength, ardour,
and time which its nature and importance demanded.   And so we will discover, under close
scrutiny of ourselves sometimes, that things legitimate, things right in themselves, things commendable, may so engross our attention, so preoccupy
our minds and so draw on our feelings, that prayer
may be omitted, or at least very little time may be
given to prayer. How easy to slip away from the
closet!   Even the Apostles had to guard themselves at that point.   How much do we need to
watch ourselves at the same place!   Things legitimate and right may become wrong when they take
the place of prayer. Things right in themselves
may become wrong things when they are allowed
to fasten themselves inordinately upon our hearts.
It is not only the sinful things which hurt prayer.
It is not alone questionable things which are to be
guarded against.   But it is things which are right

in their places, but which are allowed to sidetrack prayer and shut the closet door, often with the self-comforting plea that "we are too busy to pray."

Possibly this has had as much to do with the breaking down of family prayer in this age as any other one cause. It is at this point that family religion has decayed, and just here is one cause of the decline of the prayer meeting. Men and women are too busy with legitimate things to " give themselves to prayer." Other things are given the right of way. Prayer is set aside or made secondary. Business comes first. And this means not always that prayer is second, but that prayer is put entirely out. The Apostles drove directly at this point, and determined that even Church business should not affect their praying habits. Prayer must come first. Then would they be in deed and truth God's real agents in His world, through whom He could effectually work, because they were praying men, and thereby put themselves directly in line with His plans and purposes, which was that He works through praying men.

When the complaint came to their ears the Apostles discovered that that which they had been doing did not fully serve the divine ends of peace, gratitude, and unity, but discontent, complainings, and division were the result of their work, which had far too little prayer in it. And so prayer was put prominently to the front.

Praying men are a necessity in carrying out the divine plan for the salvation of men. God has made it so. He it is who established prayer as a divine ordinance, and this implies men are to do the praying. So that praying men are a necessity in the world. The fact that so often God has employed men of prayer to accomplish His ends clearly proves the proposition. It is altogether unnecessary to name all the instances where God used the prayers of righteous men to carry out His gracious designs. Time and space are too limited for the list. Yet one or two cases might be named. In the case of the golden calf, when God purposed to destroy the Israelites because of their great sin of idolatry, at the time when Moses was receiving the law at God's hands, the very being of Israel was imperilled, for Aaron had been swept away by the strong popular tide of unbelief and sin. All seemed lost but Moses and prayer, and prayer became more efficient and wonder-working in behalf of Israel than Aaron's magic rod. God was determined on the destruction of Israel and Aaron. His anger waxed hot. It was a fearful and a critical hour. But prayer was the levee which held back heaven's desolating fury. God's hand was held fast by the interceding of Moses, the mighty intercessor.

Moses was set on delivering Israel. It was with him a long and exhaustive struggle of praying for forty days and forty nights. Not for one moment did he relax his hold on God. Not for one moment did he quit his place at the feet of God, even for food. Not for one moment did he moderate his demand or ease his cry. Israel's existence was in the balance. Almighty God's wrath must be stayed. Israel must be saved at all hazards. And Israel was saved. Moses would not let God alone. And so, to-day, we can look back and give the credit of the present race of the Jews to the praying of Moses centuries ago.

Persevering prayer always wins; God yields to importunity and fidelity. He has no heart to say No to such praying as Moses did. Actually God's purpose to destroy Israel is changed by the praying of this man of God. It is but an illustration of how much just one praying is worth in this world, and how much depends upon him.

When Daniel, in Babylon, refused to obey the decree of the king not to ask any petition of any god or man for thirty days, he shut his eyes to the decree which would shut him off from his praying room, and refused to be deterred from calling upon God from fear of the consequences. So he " kneeled upon his knees three times a day " and prayed as he had before done, leaving it all with God as to the consequences of thus disobeying the king.

There was nothing impersonal about Daniel's praying. It always had an objective, and was an appeal to a great God, who could do all things. There was no coddling of self, nor looking after subjective or reflex influences. In the face of the dreadful decree which is to precipitate him from place and power, into the lion's den, " he kneeled upon his knees three times a day, and gave thanks to God as aforetime." The gracious result was that prayer laid its hands upon an Almighty arm, which interposed in that den of vicious, cruel lions and closed their mouths and preserved His servant Daniel, who had been true to Him and who had called upon Him for protection. Daniel's praying was an essential factor in defeating the king's de-cree and in discomfiting the wicked, envious rulers, who had set the trap for Daniel in order to destroy him and remove him from place and power in the kingdom.

II

PUTTING GOD TO WORK

": For from of old men have not heard, nor perceived by the ear, neither hath the eye seen a God beside thee who worketh for him that waiteth for him."—ISAIAH 64: 4.

THE assertion voiced in the title given this chapter is but another way of declaring that God has of His own motion placed Himself under the law of prayer, and has obligated Himself to answer the prayers of men. He has ordained prayer as a means whereby He will do things through men as they pray, which He would not otherwise do. Prayer is a specific divine appointment, an ordinance of heaven, whereby God purposes to carry out His gracious designs on earth and to execute and make efficient the plan of salvation.

When we say that prayer puts God to work, it is simply to say that man has it in his power by prayer to move God to work in His own way among men, in which way He would not work if prayer was not made. Thus while prayer moves God to work, at the same time God puts prayer to work. As God has ordained prayer, and as prayer has no existence separate from men, but involves men, then logically prayer is the one force which puts

God to work in earth's affairs through men and their prayers.

Let these fundamental truths concerning God and prayer be kept in mind in all allusions to prayer, and in all our reading of the incidents of prayer in the Scriptures.

If prayer puts God to work on earth, then, by the same token, prayerlessness rules God out of the world's affairs, and prevents Him from working. And if prayer moves God to work in this world's affairs, then prayerlessness excludes God from everything concerning men, and leaves man on earth the mere creature of circumstances, at the mercy of blind fate or without help of any kind from God. It leaves man in this world with its tremendous responsibilities and its difficult problems, and with all of its sorrows, burdens and afflictions, without any God at all. In reality the denial of prayer is a denial of God Himself, for God and prayer are so inseparable that they can never be divorced.

Prayer affects three different spheres of existence—the divine, the angelic and the human. It puts God to work, it puts angels to work, and it puts man to work. It lays its hands upon God, angels and men. What a wonderful reach there is in prayer! It brings into play the forces of heaven and earth. God, angels and men are subjects of this wonderful law of prayer, and all these have to do with the possibilities and the results of prayer. God has so far placed Himself subject to prayer that by reason of His own appointment, He

is induced to work among men in a way in which
He does not work if men do not pray. Prayer lays
hold upon God and influences Him to work. This
is the meaning of prayer as it concerns God. This
is the doctrine of prayer, or else there is nothing
whatever in prayer.

Prayer puts God to work in all things prayed
for. While man in his weakness and poverty
waits, trusts and prays, God undertakes the work.
" For from old men have not heard, nor perceived
by the ear, neither hath the eye seen a God beside
thee, which worketh for him that waiteth for thee."

Jesus Christ commits Himself to the force of
prayer. " Whatsoever ye ask in My Name," He
says, " that will I do, that the Father may be
glorified in the Son. If ye shall ask anything in
My Name, I will do it." And again: " If ye abide
in Me, and My words abide in you, ye shall ask
what ye will and it shall be done unto you."

To no other energy is the promise of God committed as to that of prayer. Upon no other force
are the purposes of God so dependent as this one
of prayer. The Word of God dilates on the results
and necessity of prayer. The work of God stays or
advances as prayer puts forth its strength. Prophets and apostles have urged the utility, force
and necessity of prayer. " I have set watchmen
upon thy walls, O Jerusalem, which shall never hold
their peace day nor night. Ye that make mention
of the Lord, keep not silence, and give him no
rest, till he establish, and till he make Jerusalem
a praise in the earth."

Prayer, with its antecedents and attendants, is the one and only condition of the final triumph of the Gospel. It is the one and only condition which honours the Father and glorifies the Son. Little and poor praying has weakened Christ's power on earth, postponed the glorious results of His reign, and retired God from His sovereignty.

Prayer puts God's work in His hands, and keeps it there. It looks to Him constantly and depends on Him implicitly to further His own cause. Prayer is but faith resting in, acting with, and leaning on and obeying God. This is why God loves it so well, why He puts all power into its hands, and why He so highly esteems men of prayer.

Every movement for the advancement of the Gospel must be created by and inspired by prayer. In all these movements of God, prayer precedes and attends as an invariable and necessary condition.

In this relation, God makes prayer identical in force and power with Himself, and says to those on earth who pray: " You are on the earth to carry on My cause. I am in heaven, the Lord of all, the Maker of all, the Holy One of all. Now whatever you need for My cause, ask Me and I will do it. Shape the future by your prayers, and all that you need for present supplies, command Me. I made heaven and earth, and all things in them. Ask largely. Open thy mouth wide, and I will fill it. It is My work which you are doing. It concerns My cause. Be prompt and full in praying.

Do not abate your asking, and I will not wince nor abate in My giving."

Everywhere in His Word God conditions His actions on prayer. Everywhere in His Word His actions and attitude are shaped by prayer. To quote all the Scriptural passages which prove the immediate, direct and personal relation of prayer to God, would be to transfer whole pages of the Scripture to this study. Man has personal relations with God. Prayer is the divinely appointed means by which man comes into direct connection with God. By His own ordinance God holds Himself bound to hear prayer. God bestows His great good on His children when they seek it along the avenue of prayer.

When Solomon closed his great prayer which he offered at the dedication of the Temple, God appeared to him, approved him, and laid down the universal principles of His action. In II Chronicles 7: 12–15 we read as follows:

" And the Lord appeared to Solomon by night and said unto him, I have heard thy prayer, and have chosen this place to myself, for a house of sacrifice.

" If I shut up heaven that there be no rain, or if I command the locusts to devour the land, or if I send pestilence among the people; if my people which are called by my name, shall humble themselves and pray, and seek my face, and turn from their wicked ways, then will I hear from heaven, and will forgive their sin, and will heal their land. Now my eyes shall be open, and my ears attentive to the prayer that is made in this place."

In His purposes concerning the Jews in the Babylonish captivity (Jer. 29: 10–13) God asserts His unfailing principles:

" For thus saith the Lord, that after seventy years be accomplished, at Babylon, I will visit you, and perform my good word toward you, in causing you to return to this place. For I know the thoughts that I think toward you, saith the Lord, thoughts of peace, and not of evil, to give you an expected end. Then shall ye call upon me, and ye shall go and pray unto me, and I will hearken unto you. And ye shall seek me and find me, when ye shall search for me with all your heart."

In Bible terminology prayer means calling upon God for things we desire, asking things of God. Thus we read: " Call upon me and I will answer thee, and will show thee great and mighty things which thou knowest not " (Jer. 33: 3). " Call upon me in the day of trouble, and I will deliver thee " (Ps. 50: 15). " Then shalt thou call, and the Lord shall answer; thou shalt cry, and he shall say, Here I am " (Isa. 58: 9).

Prayer is revealed as a direct application to God for some temporal or spiritual good. It is an appeal to God to intervene in life's affairs for the good of those for whom we pray. God is recognized as the source and fountain of all good, and prayer implies that all His good is held in His keeping for those who call upon Him in truth.

That prayer is an application to God, intercourse with God, and communion with God, comes out strongly and simply in the praying of Old Testament saints. Abraham's intercession for Sodom is a striking illustration of the nature of prayer, intercourse with God, and showing the intercessory side of prayer. The declared purpose of God to destroy Sodom confronted Abraham, and his soul within him was greatly moved because of his great interest in that fated city. His nephew and family resided there. That purpose of God must be changed. God's decree for the destruction of this evil city's inhabitants must be revoked.

It was no small undertaking which faced Abraham when he conceived the idea of beseeching God to spare Sodom. Abraham sets himself to change God's purpose and to save Sodom with the other cities of the plain. It was certainly a most difficult and delicate work for him to undertake to throw his influence with God in favour of those doomed cities so as to save them.

He bases his plea on the simple fact of the number of righteous men who could be found in Sodom, and appeals to the infinite rectitude of God not to destroy the righteous with the wicked. " That be far from thee to slay the righteous with the wicked. Shall not the Judge of all the earth do right? " With what deep self-abasement and reverence does Abraham enter upon his high and divine work! He stood before God in solemn awe, and meditation, and then drew near to God and spake. He advanced step by step in faith, in demand and urgency, and God granted every request which he made. It has been well said that " Abraham left

off asking before God left off granting." It seems
that Abraham had a kind of optimistic view of the
piety of Sodom. He scarcely expected when he
undertook this matter to have it end in failure.
He was greatly in earnest, and had every encouragement to press his case. In his final request he
surely thought that with Lot, his wife, his daugh-
ters, his sons, and his sons-in-law, he had his ten
righteous persons for whose sake God would spare
the city. But alas! The count failed when the
final test came. There were not ten righteous people in that large population.

But this was true. If he did not save Sodom by
his importunate praying, the purposes of God were
stayed for a season, and possibly had not Abraham's goodness of heart over-estimated the number
of pious people in that devoted city, God might
have saved it had he reduced his figures still
further.

This is a representative case illustrative of Old
Testament praying, and disclosing God's mode of
working through prayer. It shows further how
God is moved to work in answer to prayer in this
world even when it comes to changing His purposes concerning a sinful community. This praying of Abraham was no mere performance, no dull,
lifeless ceremony, but an earnest plea, a strong
advocacy, to secure a desired end, to have an influence, one person with another person.

How full of meaning is this series of remarkable
intercessions made by Abraham! Here we have
arguments designed to convince God, and pleas to

persuade God to change His purpose. We see deep humility, but holy boldness as well, perseverance, and advances made based on victory in each petition. Here we have enlarged asking encouraged by enlarged answers. God stays and answers as long as Abraham stays and asks. To Abraham God is existent, approachable, and all powerful, but at the same time He defers to men, acts favourably on their desires, and grants them favours asked for. Not to pray is a denial of God, a denial of His existence, a denial of His nature, and a denial of His purposes toward mankind.

God has specifically to do with prayer promises in their breadth, certainty and limitations. Jesus Christ presses us into the presence of God with these prayer promises, not only by the assurance that God will answer, but that no other being but God can answer. He presses us to God because only in this way can we move God to take a hand in earth's affairs, and induce Him to intervene in our behalf.

"All things whatsoever ye ask in prayer, believing, ye shall receive," says Jesus, and this all-comprehensive condition not only presses us to pray for all things, everything great and small, but it sets us on and shuts us up to God, for who but God can cover the illimitable of universal things, and can assure us certainly of receiving the very thing for which we may ask in all the Thesaurus of earthly and heavenly good?

It is Jesus Christ, the Son of God, who makes demands on us to pray, and it is He who puts Himself and all He has so fully in the answer. He it is who puts Himself at our service and answers our demands when we pray.

And just as He puts Himself and the Father at our command in prayer, to come directly into our lives and to work for our good, so also does He engage to answer the demands of two or more believers who are agreed as touching any one thing. "If two of you shall agree on earth as touching anything, that they shall ask, it shall be done for them of my Father which is in heaven." None but God could put Himself in a covenant so binding as that, for God only could fulfil such a promise and could reach to its exacting and all controlling demands. God only can answer for the promises.

God needs prayer, and man needs prayer, too. It is indispensable to God's work in this world, and is essential to getting God to work in earth's affairs. So God binds men to pray by the most solemn obligations. God commands men to pray, and so not to pray is plain disobedience to an imperative command of Almighty God. Prayer is such a condition without which the graces, the salvation and the good of God are not bestowed on men. Prayer is a high privilege, a royal prerogative and manifold and eternal are the losses by failure to exercise it. Prayer is the great, universal force to advance God's cause; the reverence which hallows God's name; the ability to do God's will, and the establishment of God's kingdom in the hearts of the children of men. These, and their coincidents and agencies, are created and affected by prayer.

One of the constitutional enforcements of the Gospel is prayer. Without prayer, the Gospel can neither be preached effectively, promulgated faithfully, experienced in the heart, nor be practiced in the life. And for the very simple reason that by leaving prayer out of the catalogue of religious duties, we leave God out, and His work cannot progress without Him.

The movements which God purposed under Cyrus, king of Persia, prophesied about by Isaiah many years before Cyrus was born, are conditioned on prayer. God declares His purpose, power, independence and defiance of obstacles in the way of Him carrying out those purposes. His omnipotent and absolutely infinite power is set to encourage prayer. He has been ordering all events, directing all conditions, and creating all things, that He might answer prayer, and then turns Himself over to His praying ones to be commanded. And then all the results and power He holds in His hands will be bestowed in lavish and unmeasured munificence to carry out prayers and to make prayer the mightiest energy in the world.

The passage in Isaiah (chap. 46) is too lengthy to be quoted in its entirety but it is well worth reading. It closes with such strong words as these, words about prayer, which are the climax of all which God has been saying concerning His purposes in connection with Cyrus:

" Thus saith the Lord, the Holy One of Israel, and his Maker: Ask me of things to come, concerning my sons, and concerning the work of my hands, command ye me. I have made the earth, and created man upon it; I, even my hands, have stretched out the heavens, and all their hosts have I commanded."

In the conclusion of the history of Job, we see how God intervenes in behalf of Job and calls upon his friends to present themselves before Job that he may pray for them. " My wrath is kindled against thee and against thy two friends," is God's statement, with the further words added, " My servant Job shall pray for you, for him will I accept," a striking illustration of God intervening to deliver Job's friends in answer to Job's prayer.

We have heretofore spoken of prayer affecting God, angels and men. Christ wrote nothing while living. Memoranda, notes, sermon writing, sermon making, were alien to Him. Autobiography was not to His taste. The Revelation of John was His last utterance. In that book we have pictured the great importance, the priceless value, and the high position which prayer obtains in the movements, history, and unfolding progress of God's Church in this world. We have this picture in Revelation 8: 3, disclosing the interest the angels in heaven have in the prayers of the saints and in accomplishing the answers to those prayers:

" And another angel came and stood at the altar, having a golden censer, and there was given unto him much incense, that he should offer it with the prayers of all saints, upon the golden altar which was before the throne. And the smoke of the incense which came

with the prayers of the saints, ascended up before God,
out of the angel's hand. And the angel took the censer,
and filled it with fire of the altar, and cast it into the
earth, and there were voices, and thunderings and light-
nings and an earthquake."

Translated into the prose of everyday life, these
words show how the capital stock by which heaven
carries on the business of salvation under Christ, is
made up of the prayers of God's saints on earth,
and discloses how these prayers in flaming power
come back to earth and produce its mighty com-
motions, influences and revolutions.

Praying men are essential to Almighty God in all
His plans and purposes. God's secrets, councils
and cause have never been committed to prayerless
men. Neglect of prayer has always brought loss
of faith, loss of love, and loss of prayer. Failure
to pray has been the baneful, inevitable cause of
backsliding and estrangement from God. Prayerless men have stood in the way of God fulfilling His
Word and doing His will on earth. They tie the
divine hands and interfere with God in His gracious designs. As praying men are a help to God,
so prayerless men are a hindrance to Him.

We press the Scriptural view of the necessity of
prayer, even at the cost of repetition. The subject
is too important for repetition to weaken or tire,
too vital to be trite or tame. We must feel it anew.
The fires of prayer have burned low. Ashes and
not flames are on its altars.

No insistence in the Scriptures is more pressing

than prayer. No exhortation is oftener reiterated, none is more hearty, none is more solemn and stirring, than to pray. No principle is more strongly and broadly declared than that which urges us to prayer. There is no duty to which we are more strongly obliged than the obligation to pray. There is no command more imperative and insistent than that of praying. Art thou praying in everything without ceasing, in the closet, hidden from the eyes of men, and praying always and everywhere? That is the personal, pertinent and all-important question for every soul.

Many instances occur in God's Word showing that God intervenes in this world in answer to prayer. Nothing is clearer when the Bible is consulted than that Almighty God is brought directly into the things of this world by the praying of His people. Jonah flees from duty and takes ship for a distant port. But God follows him, and by a strange providence this disobedient prophet is cast out of the vessel, and the God who sent him to Nineveh prepares a fish to swallow him. In the fish's belly he cries out to the God against whom he had sinned, and God intervenes and causes the fish to vomit Jonah out on dry land. Even the fishes of the great deep are subject to the law of prayer.

Likewise the birds of the air are brought into subjection to this same law. Elijah had foretold to Ahab the coming of that prolonged drouth, and food and even water became scarce. God sent him to the brook Cherith, and said unto him, " It shall

be that thou shalt drink of the brook, and I have
commanded the ravens to feed thee there. And the
ravens brought bread and flesh in the morning,
and bread and flesh in the evening." Can any one
doubt that this man of God, who later on shut up
and opened the rain clouds by prayer was not praying about this time, when so much was at stake?
God interposed among the birds of the air this time
and strangely moved them to take care of His servant so that he would not want food and water.

David in an evil hour, instead of listening to the
advice of Joab, his prime minister, yielded to the
suggestion of Satan, and counted the people, which
displeased God. So God told him to choose one of
three evils as a retribution for his folly and sin.
Pestilence came among the people in violent form,
and David betakes himself to prayer.

" And David said unto God, Is it not I that commanded the people to be numbered? Even I it is that
hath sinned and done evil indeed. But as for these
sheep, what have they done? Let thy hand, I pray
thee, O Lord my God, be on me, and on my father's
house; but not on thy people, that they should be
plagued " (I Chron. 21: 17).

And though God had been greatly grieved at
David for numbering Israel, yet He could not resist
this appeal of a penitent and prayerful spirit, and
God was moved by prayer to put His hand on the
springs of disease and stop the fearful plague. God
was put to work by David's prayer.

Numbers of other cases could be named. These are sufficient. God seems to have taken great pains in His divine revelation to men to show how He interferes in earth's affairs in answer to the praying of His saints.

The question might arise just here in some over-critical minds as to the so-called " laws of nature," who are not strong believers in prayer, as if there was a conflict between what they call the " laws of nature " and the law of prayer. These people make nature a sort of imaginary god entirely separate of Almighty God. What is nature anyway? It is but the creation of God, the Maker of all things. And what are the " laws of nature " but the laws of God, through which He governs the material world. As the law of prayer is also the law of God, there cannot possibly be any conflict between the two sets of laws, but all must work in perfect harmony. Prayer does not violate any natural law. God may set aside one law for the higher working of another law, and this He may do when He answers prayer. Or Almighty God may answer prayer working through the course of natural law. But whether or not we understand it, God is over and above all nature, and can and will answer prayer in a wise, intelligent and just manner, even though man may not comprehend it. So that in no sense is there any discord or conflict between God's several laws when God is induced to interfere with human affairs in answer to prayer.

In this connection another word might be said. We used the form of words to which there can be no objection, that prayer does certain things, but this of course implies not that prayer as a human means accomplishes anything, but that prayer only accomplishes things instrumentally. Prayer is the instrument, God is the efficient and active agent. So that prayer in itself does not interfere in earth's affairs, but prayer in the hands of men moves God to intervene and do things, which He would not otherwise do if prayer was not used as the instrument.

It is as we say, " faith hath saved thee," by which is simply meant that God through the faith of the sinner saves him, faith being only the instrument used by the sinner which brings salvation to him.

III

THE NECESSITY FOR PRAYING MEN

"Praying always with all prayer and supplication in the Spirit and watching thereunto with all perseverance and supplication for all saints."—EPHESIANS 6: 18.

"Withal praying for us also that God would open unto us a door of utterance to speak the mystery of Christ, for which I am in bonds: that I may make it manifest as I ought to speak."
—COLOSSIANS 4: 3.

ONE of the crying things of our day is for men whose faith, prayers and study of the Word of God have been vitalized, and a transcript of that Word is written on their hearts, and who will give it forth as the incorruptible seed that liveth and abideth forever. Nothing more is needed to clear up the haze by which a critical unfaith has eclipsed the Word of God than the fidelity of the pulpit in its unwavering allegiance to the Bible and the fearless proclamation of its truth. Without this the standard-bearer fails, and wavering and confusion all along the ranks follow. The pulpit has wrought its mightiest work in the days of its unswerving loyalty to the Word of God.

In close connection with this, must we have men of prayer, men in high and low places who hold to and practice Scriptural praying. While the pulpit must hold to its unswerving loyalty to the Word of

God, it must, at the same time, be loyal to the doctrine of prayer which that same Word illustrates and enforces upon mankind.

Schools, colleges and education considered simply as such cannot be regarded as being leaders in carrying forward the work of God's kingdom in the world. They have neither the right, the will nor the power to do the work. This is to be accomplished by the preached Word, delivered in the power of the Holy Ghost sent down from heaven, sown with prayerful hands, and watered with the tears of praying hearts. This is the divine law, and so " nominated in the bond." We are shut up and sealed to it—we would follow the Lord.

Men are demanded for the great work of soul saving, and men must go. It is no angelic or impersonal force which is needed. Human hearts baptized with the spirit of prayer, must bear the burden of this message, and human tongues on fire as the result of earnest, persistent prayer, must declare the Word of God to dying men.

The Church, to-day, needs praying men to execute her solemn and pressing responsibility to meet the fearful crisis which is facing her. The crying need of the times is for men, in increased numbers—God-fearing men, praying men, Holy-Ghost men, men who can endure hardness, who will count not their lives dear unto themselves, but count all things but dross for the excellency of the knowledge of Jesus Christ, the Saviour. The men who are so greatly needed in this age of the Church are those who have learned the business of praying,

—learned it upon their knees, learned it in the need and agony of their own hearts.

Praying men are the one commanding need of this day, as of all other days, in which God is to have or make a showing. Men who pray are, in reality, the only religious men, and it takes a full-measured man to pray. Men of prayer are the only men who do or can represent God in this world. No cold, irreligious, prayerless man can claim the right. They misrepresent God in all His work, and all His plans. Praying men are the only men who have influence with God, the only kind of men to whom God commits Himself and His Gospel. Praying men are the only men in which the Holy Spirit dwells, for the Holy Spirit and prayer go hand-in-hand. The Holy Spirit never descends upon prayerless men. He never fills them, He never empowers them. There is nothing whatever in common between the Spirit of God and men who do not pray. The Spirit dwells only in a prayer atmosphere.

In doing God's work there is no substitute for praying. The men of prayer cannot be displaced with other kinds of men. Men of financial skill, men of education, men of worldly influence—none of these can possibly be put in substitution for the men of prayer. The life, the vigour, the motive-power of God's work is formed by praying men. A vitally diseased heart is not a more fearful symptom of approaching death than non-praying men are of spiritual atrophy.

The men to whom Jesus Christ committed the fortunes and destiny of His Church were men of prayer. To no other kind of men has God ever committed Himself in this world. The Apostles were preëminently men of prayer. They gave themselves to prayer. They made praying their chief business. It was first in point of importance and first in results. God never has, and He never will, commit the weighty interests of His kingdom to prayerless men, who do not make prayer a conspicuous and controlling factor in their lives. Men never rise to any eminence of piety who do not pray. Men of piety are always men of prayer. Men are never noted for the simplicity and strength of their faith who are not preëminently men of prayer. Piety flourishes nowhere so rapidly and so rankly as in the closet. The closet is the garden of faith.

The Apostles allowed no duty, however sacred, to so engage them as to infringe upon their time and prevent them from making prayer the main thing. The Word of God was ministered by apostolic fidelity and zeal. It was spoken by men with apostolic commissions and whose heads the fiery tongues of Pentecost had baptized. The Word was pointless and powerless without they were freshly endued with power by continuous and mighty prayer. The seed of God's Word must be saturated in prayer to make it germinate. It grows readier and roots deeper when it is prayer-soaked.

The Apostles were praying men, themselves. They were teachers of prayer, and trained their disciples in the school of prayer. They urged prayer upon their disciples not only that they might attain to the loftiest eminence of faith, but that they might be the most powerful factors in advancing God's kingdom.

Jesus Christ was the divinely appointed leader of God's people, and no one thing in His life proves His eminent fitness for that office so fully as His habit of prayer. Nothing is more suggestive of thought than Christ's continual praying, and nothing is more conspicuous about Him than prayer. His campaigns were arranged, His victories gained, in the struggles and communion of His all-night praying. His praying rent the heavens. Moses and Elijah and the Transfiguration glory waited on His praying. His miracles and His teaching had their force from the same source. Gethsemane's praying crimsoned Calvary with serenity and glory. His prayer makes the history and hastens the triumphs of His Church. What an inspiration and command to prayer is Christ's life! What a comment on its worth! How He shames our lives by His praying!

Like all His followers who have drawn God nearer to the world and lifted the world nearer to God, Jesus was the man of prayer, made of God a leader and commander to His people. His leadership was one of prayer. A great leader He was, because He was great in prayer. All great leaders for God have fashioned their leadership in the wrestlings of their closets. Many great men have led and moulded the Church who have not been great in prayer, but they were great only in their plans, great for their opinions, great for their organization, great by natural gifts, by the force of genius or of character. However, they were not great for God. But Jesus Christ was a great leader for God. His was the great leadership of great praying. God was in His leadership greatly because prayer was in it greatly. We might just well express the wish that we be taught by Him to pray, and to pray more and more.

Herein has been the secret of the men of prayer in the past history of the Church. Their hearts were after God, their desires were on Him, their prayers were addressed to Him. They communed with Him, sought nothing of the world, sought great things of God, wrestled with Him, conquered all opposing forces, and opened up the channel of faith deep and broad between them and heaven. And all this was done by the use of prayer. Holy meditations, spiritual desires, heavenly drawings, swayed their intellects, enriched their emotions, and filled and enlarged their hearts. And all this was so because they were first of all men of prayer.

The men who have thus communed with God and who have sought after Him with their whole hearts, have always risen to consecrated eminence, and no man has ever risen to this eminence whose flames of holy desire have not all been dead to the world and all aglow for God and heaven. Nor have they ever risen to the heights of the higher spiritual experiences unless prayer and the spirit of prayer have been conspicuous and controlling factors in their lives.

The entire consecration of many of God's children stands out distinctly like towering mountain-peaks. Why is this? How did they ascend to these heights? What brought them so near to God? What made them so Christ-like? The answer is easy—prayer. They prayed much, prayed long, and drank deeper and deeper still. They asked, they sought, and they knocked, till heaven opened its richest inner treasures of grace to them. Prayer was the Jacob's Ladder by which they scaled those holy and blessed heights, and the way by which the angels of God came down to and ministered to them.

The men of spiritual mould and might always value prayer. They took time to be alone with God. Their praying was no hurried performance. They had many serious wants to be relieved, and many weighty pleas they had to offer. Many large supplies they must secure. They had to do much silent waiting before God, and much patient iteration and reiteration to utter to Him. Prayer was the only channel through which supplies came, and was the only way to utter pleas. The only acceptable waiting before God of which they knew anything was prayer. They valued praying. It was more precious to them than all jewels, more excellent than any good, more to be valued than the greatest good of earth. They esteemed it, valued it, prized it, and did it. They pressed it to its farthest limits, tested its greatest results, and secured its most glorious patrimony. To them prayer was the one great thing to be appreciated and used.

The Apostles above everything else were praying men, and left the impress of their prayer example and teaching upon the early Church. But the Apostles are dead, and times and men have changed. They have no successors by official entail or heirship. And the times have no commission to make other apostles. Prayer is the entail to spiritual and apostolical leadership. Unfortunately the times are not prayerful times. God's cause just now needs very greatly praying leaders. Other things may be needed, but above all else this is the crying demand of these times and the urgent first need of the Church.

This is the day of great wealth in the Church and of wonderful material resources. But unfortunately the affluence of material resources is a great enemy and a severe hindrance to strong spiritual forces. It is an invariable law that the presence of attractive and potent material forces creates a trust in them, and by the same inevitable law, creates distrust in the spiritual forces of the Gospel. They are two masters which cannot be served at one and the same time. For just in proportion as the mind is fixed on one, will it be drawn away from the other. The days of great financial prosperity in the Church have not been days of great religious prosperity. Moneyed men and praying men are not synonymous terms.

Paul in the second chapter of his First Epistle to Timothy, emphasizes the need of men to pray. Church leaders in his estimation are to be conspicuous for their praying. Prayer ought and must of necessity shape their characters, and must be one of their distinguishing characteristics. Prayer ought to be one of their most powerful elements, so much so that it cannot be hid. Prayer ought to make Church leaders notable. Character, official duty, reputation and life, all should be shaped by prayer. The mighty forces of prayer lie in its praying leaders in a marked way. The standing obligation to pray rests in a peculiar sense on Church leaders. Wise will the Church be to discover this prime truth and give prominence to it.

It may be laid down as an axiom, that God needs, first of all, leaders in the Church who will be first in prayer, men with whom prayer is habitual and characteristic, men who know the primacy of prayer. But even more than a habit of prayer, and more than prayer being characteristic of them, Church leaders are to be *impregnated* with prayer —men whose lives are made and moulded by prayer, whose heart and life are made up of prayer. These are the men—the only men—God can use in the furtherance of His kingdom and the implanting of His message in the hearts of men.

IV

GOD'S NEED OF MEN WHO PRAY

"We do what He commands. We go where He wants us to go. We speak what He wants us to speak. His will is our law. His pleasure our joy. He is, to-day, seeking the lost and He would have us seek with Him. He is shepherding the lambs and He wants our cooperation. He is opening doors in heathen lands, and He wants our money and our prayers."—ANON.

WE proceed now to declare that it demands prayer-leadership to hold the Church to God's aims, and to fit it for God's uses. Prayer-leadership preserves the spirituality of the Church, just as prayerless leaders make for unspiritual conditions. The Church is not spiritual simply by the mere fact of its existence, nor by its vocation. It is not held to its sacred vocation by generation, nor by succession. Like the new birth, " It is not of blood, neither of the flesh, nor of the will of man, but of God."

The Church is not spiritual simply because it is concerned and deals in spiritual values. It may hold its confirmations by the thousand, it may multiply its baptisms, and administer its sacraments innumerable times, and yet be as far from fulfilling its true mission as human conditions can make it.

This present world's general attitude retires prayer to insignificance and obscurity. By it, salvation and eternal life are put in the background. It cannot be too often affirmed, therefore, that the prime need of the Church is not men of money nor men of brains, but men of prayer. Leaders in the realm of religious activity are to be judged by their praying habits, and not by their money or social position. Those who must be placed in the forefront of the Church's business, must be, first of all, men who know how to pray.

God does not conduct His work, solely, with men of education or of wealth or of business capacity. Neither can He carry on His work through men of large intellects or of great culture, nor yet through men of great social eminence and influence. All these can be made to count provided they are not regarded as being primary. These men, by the simple fact of these qualities and conditions, cannot lead in God's work nor control His cause. Men of prayer, before anything else, are indispensable to the furtherance of the kingdom of God on earth. No other sort will fit in the scheme or do the deed. Men, great and influential in other things, but small in prayer, cannot do the work Almighty God has set out for His Church to do in this, His world.

Men who represent God and who stand here in His stead, men who are to build up His kingdom in this world, must be in an eminent sense men of prayer. Whatever else they may have, whatever else they may lack, they must be men of prayer. Having everything else and lacking prayer, they must fail. Having prayer and lacking all else, they can succeed. Prayer must be the most conspicuous and the most potent factor in the character and conduct of men who undertake divine commission. God's business requires men who are versed in the business of praying.

It must be kept in mind that the praying to which the disciples of Christ is called by Scriptural authority and enforcement, is a valorous calling, for manly men. The men God wants and upon whom He depends, must work at prayer just as they work at their worldly calling. They must follow this business of praying *through,* just as they do their secular pursuits. Diligence, perseverance, heartiness, and courage, must all be in it if it is to succeed.

Everything secured by Gospel promise, defined by Gospel measure, and represented by Gospel treasure are to be found in prayer. All heights are scaled by it, all doors are opened to it, all victories are gained through it, and all grace distills on it. Heaven has all its good and all its help for men who pray.

How marked and strong is the injunction of Christ which sends men from the parade of public giving and praying to the privacy of their closets, where with shut doors, and in encircling silence they are alone in prayer with God!

In all ages, those who have carried out the divine will on the earth, have been men of prayer. The days of prayer are God's halcyon days. His heart, His oath, and His glory are committed to one issuance—that every knee should bow to Him.

The day of the Lord, in a preëminent sense, will be a day of universal prayer.

God's cause does not suffer through lack of divine ability, but by reason of the lack of prayerability in man. God's action is just as much bound up in prayer at this time, as it was when He said to Abimelech, "Abraham shall pray for thee, and thou shalt live." So also it was when God said to Job's friends, "My servant Job shall pray for you, for him will I accept."

God's great plan for the redemption of mankind is as much bound up to prayer for its prosperity and success as when the decree creating the movement was issued from the Father, bearing on its frontage the imperative, universal and eternal condition, "Ask of me, and I will give thee the heathen for thy inheritance and the uttermost part of the earth for thy possession."

In many places an alarming state of things has come to pass, in that the many who are enrolled in our churches are not praying men and women. Many of those occupying prominent positions in church life are not praying men. It is greatly to be feared that much of the work of the Church is being done by those who are perfect strangers to the closet. Small wonder that the work does not succeed.

While it may be true that many in the Church say prayers, it is equally true that their praying is of the stereotyped order. Their prayers may be charged with sentiment, but they are tame, timid, and without fire or force. Even this sort of praying is done by a few straggling men to be found at prayer-meetings. Those whose names are to be found bulking large in our great Church assemblies are not men noted for their praying habits. Yet the entire fabric of the work in which they are engaged has, perforce, to depend on the adequacy of prayer. This fact is similar to the crisis which would be created were a country to have to admit in the face of an invading foe that it cannot fight and have no knowledge of the weapons whereby war is to be waged.

In all God's plans for human redemption, He proposes that men *pray*. The men are to pray in every place, in the church, in the closet, in the home, on sacred days and on secular days. All things and everything are dependent on the measure of men's praying.

Prayer is the genius and mainspring of life. We pray as we live; we live as we pray. Life will never be finer than the quality of the closet. The mercury of life will rise only by the warmth of the closet. Persistent non-praying eventually will depress life below zero.

To measure and weigh the conditions of prayer, is readily to discover why men do not pray in larger numbers. The conditions are so perfect, so blessed, that it is a rare character who can meet them. A heart all love, a heart that holds even its enemies in loving contemplation and prayerful concern, a heart from which all bitterness, revenge and envy are purged—how rare! Yet this is the only condition of mind and heart in which a man can expect to command the efficacy of prayer.

There are certain conditions laid down for authentic praying. Men are to pray, " lifting up holy hands "; hands here being the symbol of life. Hands unsoiled by stains of evil doing are the emblem of a life unsoiled by sin. Thus are men to come into the presence of God, thus are they to approach the throne of the Highest, where they can " obtain mercy and find grace to help in time of need." Here, then, is one reason why men do not pray. They are too worldly in heart and too secular in life to enter the closet; and even though they enter there, they cannot offer the " fervent, effectual prayer of the righteous man, which availeth much."

Again, " hands " are the symbols of supplication. Outstretched hands stand for an appeal for help. It is the silent yet eloquent attitude of a helpless soul standing before God, appealing for mercy and grace. " Hands," too, are symbols of activity, power and conduct. Hands outstretched to God in prayer must be " holy hands," unstained hands. The word " holy " here means undefiled, unspotted, untainted, and religiously observing every obligation. How far remote is all this from the character of the sin-loving, worldly-minded, fleshly disposed men, soiled by fleshly lusts, spotted by worldly indulgence, unholy in heart and conduct! " He who seeks equity must do equity," is the maxim of earthly courts. So he who seeks God's good gifts must practice God's good deeds. This is the maxim of heavenly courts.

Prayer is sensitive, and always affected by the character and conduct of him who prays. Water cannot rise above its own level, and a spotless prayer cannot flow from a spotted heart. Straight praying is never born of crooked conduct. The men, what men are, behind their praying, that gives character to their supplication. The craven heart cannot do brave praying. Soiled men cannot make clean, pure supplication.

It is neither words, nor thoughts nor ideas, nor feelings, which shape praying, but character and conduct. Men must walk in upright fashion in order to be able to pray well. Bad character and unrighteous living break down praying until it becomes a mere shibboleth. Praying takes its tone and vigour from the life of the man or the woman exercising it. When character and conduct are at a low ebb, praying can but barely live, much less thrive.

The man of prayer, whether layman or preacher, is God's right-hand man. In the realm of spiritual affairs, he creates conditions, inaugurates movements, brings things to pass.

By the fact and condition of their creation and redemption, all men are under obligation to pray. Every man *can* pray, and every man *should* pray. But when it comes to the affairs of the Kingdom, let it be said, at once, that a prayerless man in the Church of God is like a paralyzed organ of the physical body. He is out of place in the communion of saints, out of harmony with God, and out of accord with His purposes for mankind. A prayerless man handicaps the vigour and life of the whole system like a demoralized soldier is a menace to the force of which he forms part, in the day of battle. The absence of prayer lessens all the life-forces of the soul, cripples faith, sets aside holy living, shuts out heaven. Between praying saints and non-praying men, in Holy Scripture, the line is sharply drawn. Of Fletcher of Madeley— one of the praying saints—it is written that

"He was far more abundant in his public labours than the greater part of his companions in the holy ministry. Yet these bore but little proportion to those internal exercises of prayer and supplication to which he was wholly given up in private, which were almost uninterruptedly maintained from hour to hour. He lived in the spirit of prayer, and whatever employment in which he was engaged, this spirit of prayer was constantly manifested through them all.

"Without this he neither formed any design, nor entered upon any duty. Without this he neither read nor conversed. Without this, he neither visited nor received a visitor. There have been seasons of supplications in which he appeared to be carried out far beyond the ordinary limits of devotion, when, like his Lord upon the Mount of Transfiguration, while he continued to pour out his mighty prayer, the fashion of his countenance has been changed, and his face has appeared as the face of an angel."

O God, raise up more men of praying like John Fletcher! How we do need, in this our day, men through whom God can work!

V

PRAYERLESS CHRISTIANS

" If there was ever a time when Peter, James and John needed
to remain awake it was in Gethsemane. If James had persisted
in keeping awake it might have saved his decapitation a few years
later. If Peter had stirred himself to really intercede for himself
and others he would not have denied his Christ that night in the
palace of Caiaphas."—H. W. HODGE.

THERE is great need in this day for Christian business men to inform their mundane affairs with the spirit of prayer. There is a great army of successful merchants of almost every kind who are members of Christ's Church and it is high time these men attended to this matter. This is but another version of the phrase, " putting God into business," the realization and restraint of His presence and of His fear in all the secularities of life. We need the atmosphere of the prayer-closet to pervade our public salesrooms and counting-houses. The sanctity of prayer is needed to impregnate business. We need the spirit of Sunday carried over to Monday and continued until Saturday. But this cannot be done by prayerless men, but by men of prayer. We need business men to go about their concerns with the same reverence and responsibility with which they enter the closet. Men are badly needed who are devoid of greed, but who, with all their hearts, carry God with them into the secular affairs of life.

Men of the world imagine prayer to be too impotent a thing to come into rivalry with business methods and worldly practices. Against such a misleading doctrine Paul sets the whole commands of God, the loyalty to Jesus Christ, the claims of pious character, and the demands of the salvation of the world. Men must pray, and put strength and heart into their praying. This is part of the primary business of life, and to it God has called men, first of all.

Praying men are God's agents on earth, the representative of government of heaven, set to a specific task on the earth. While it is true that the Holy Spirit, the angels of God, are agents of God in carrying forward the redemption of the human race, yet among them there must be praying men. For such men God has great use. He can make much of them, and in the past has done wonderful things through them. These are His instruments in carrying out God's great purposes on the earth. They are God's messengers, His watchmen, shepherds, workmen, who need not be ashamed. Fully equipped for the great work to which they are appointed, they honour God and bless the world.

Above all things beside, Christian men and women must, primarily, be leaders in prayer. No matter how conspicuous they may be in other activities, they fail if they are not conspicuous in prayer. They must give their brain and heart to prayer. Men who make and shape the program of Christ's Church, who map out its line of activity, should, themselves, be shaped and made by prayer. Men controlling the Church finances, her thought, her action—should all be men of prayer.

The progress to consummation of God's work in this world has two basic principles—God's ability to give and man's ability to ask. Failure in either one is fatal to the success of God's work on earth. God's inability to do or to give would put an end to redemption. Man's failure to pray would, just as surely, set a limit to the plan. But God's ability to do and to give has never failed and *cannot* fail; but man's ability to ask can fail, and often does. Therefore the slow progress which is being made toward the realization of a world won for Christ lies entirely with man's limited asking. There is need for the entire Church of God, on the earth, to betake itself to prayer. The Church upon its knees would bring heaven upon the earth.

The wonderful ability of God to do for us is thus expressed by Paul in one of his most comprehensive statements, " And God is able to make all grace abound toward you," he says, " that ye, always, having all sufficiency in all things, may abound to every good work."

Study, I pray you, that remarkable statement— " God is able to make all grace abound." That is, He is able to give such sufficiency, that we may abound—overflow—to every good work. Why are we not more fully fashioned after this overflowing order? The answer is—lack of prayer-ability. " We have not because we ask not." We are feeble, weak and impoverished because of our failure to pray. God is restrained in doing because we are restrained by reason of our non-praying. All failures in securing heaven are traceable to lack of prayer or misdirected petition.

Prayer must be broad in its scope—it must plead for others. Intercession for others is the hall-mark of all true prayer. When prayer is confined to self and to the sphere of one's personal needs, it dies by reason of its littleness, narrowness and selfishness. Prayer must be broad and unselfish or it will perish. Prayer is the soul of a man stirred to plead with God for men. In addition to being interested in the eternal interests of one's own soul it must, in its very nature, be concerned for the spiritual and eternal welfare of others. One's ability to pray for self, finds its climax in the compassion its concern expresses for others.

In I Timothy 1, the Apostle Paul urges with singular and specific emphasis, that those who occupy positions of influence and places of authority, are to give themselves to prayer. " I will, therefore, that the men pray everywhere." This is the high calling of the men of the Church, and no calling is so engaging, so engrossing and so valuable that we can afford to relieve Christian men from the all-important vocation of secret prayer. Nothing whatever can take the place of prayer. Nothing whatever can atone for the neglect of praying. This is uppermost, first in point of importance and first in point of time. No man is so high in position, or in grace, to be exempt from an obligation to pray. No man is too big to pray, no matter who he is, nor what office he fills. The king on his throne is as much obligated to pray as the peasant in his cottage. None is so high and exalted in this world or so lowly and obscure as to be excused from praying. The help of every one is needed in prosecuting the work of God, and the prayer of each praying man helps to swell the aggregate. The leaders in place, in gifts and in authority are to be chiefs in prayer.

Civil and Church rulers shape the affairs of this world. And so civil and Church rulers themselves need to be shaped personally in spirit, heart and conduct, in truth and righteousness, by the prayers of God's people. This is in direct line with Paul's words:

" I exhort therefore," he says, " that, first of all, supplications, prayers, intercessions, and giving of thanks be made for all men, for rulers and all that are in authority."

It is a sad day for righteousness when church politics instead of holy praying, shapes the administration of the Kingdom and elevates men to place and power. Why pray for all men? Because God wills the salvation of all men. God's children on earth must link their prayers to God's will. Prayer is to carry out the will of God. God wills the salvation of all men. His heart is set on this one thing. Our prayers must be the creation and exponent of God's will. We are to grasp humanity in our praying as God grasps humanity in His love, His interest and His plans to redeem humanity. Our sympathies, prayers, wrestling and ardent desires must run parallel with the will of God, broad, generous, world-wide and Godlike. The Christian man must in all things, first of all, be conformed to the will of God, but nowhere shall this royal devotion be more evident than in the salvation of the race of men. This high partnership with God, as His vicegerents on earth, is to have its fullest, richest, and most efficient exercise in prayer for all men.

Men are to pray for all men, are to pray especially for rulers in Church and state, " that we may lead a quiet and peaceable life in all godliness and honesty." Peace on the outside and peace on the inside. Praying calms disturbing forces, allays tormenting fears, brings conflict to an end. Prayer tends to do away with turmoil. But even if there be external conflicts, it is well to have deep peace within the citadel of the soul. " That we may lead a quiet and peaceable life." Prayer brings the inner calm and furnishes the outward tranquillity. Praying rulers and praying subjects were they world-wide would allay turbulent forces, make wars to cease, and peace to reign.

Men must pray for all men that we may lead lives " in all godliness and honesty." That is with godliness and gravity. Godliness is to be like God. It is to be godly, to have God-likeness, having the image of God stamped upon the inner nature, and showing the same likeness in conduct and in temper. Almighty God is the very highest model, and to be like Him is to possess the highest character. Prayer moulds us into the image of God, and at the same time tends to mould others into the same image just in proportion as we pray for others. Prayer means to be God-like, and to be God-like is to love Christ and love God, to be one with the Father and the Son in spirit, character and conduct. Prayer means to stay with God till you are like Him. Prayer makes a godly man, and puts within him " the mind of Christ," the mind of humility, of self-surrender, of service, of pity, and of prayer. If we really pray, we will become more like God, or else we will quit praying.

" Men are to pray everywhere," in the closet, in the prayer-meeting, about the family altar, and to do it, " lifting up holy hands, without wrath and doubting." Here is not only the obligation laid upon the men to pray, but instructions as to how they should pray. " Men must pray without wrath." That is, without bitterness against their neighbours or brethren; without the obstinacy and pertinacity of a strong will, and hard feelings, without an evil desire or emotion kindled by nature's fires in the carnal nature. Praying is not to be done by these questionable things, nor in company with such evil feelings, but " without " them, aloof and entirely separate from them. This is the sort of praying the men are called upon to do, the sort which God hears and the kind which prevails with God and accomplishes things. Such praying in the hands of Christian men become divine agencies in God's hands for carrying on God's gracious purposes and executing His designs in redemption.

Prayer has a higher origin than man's nature. This is true whether man's nature as separate from the angelic nature, or man's carnal nature unrenewed and unchanged be meant. Prayer does not originate in the realms of the carnal mind. Such a nature is entirely foreign to prayer simply because "the carnal mind is enmity against God." It is by the new Spirit that we pray, the new spirit sweetened by the sugar of heaven perfumed with the fragrance of the upper world, and invigorated by a breath from the crystal sea. The " new spirit " is native to the skies, panting after the heavenly things, inspired by the breath of God. It is the praying temper from which all the old juices of the carnal, unregenerate nature have been expelled, and the fire of God has created the flame which has consumed worldly lusts, and the juices of the Spirit have been injected into the soul, and the praying is entirely divorced from wrath.

Men are also to pray " without doubting." The Revised Version puts it, " without disputings." Faith in God, belief in God's Word, they must have " without question." No doubting or disputing must be in the mind. There must be no opinions, nor hesitancy, no questioning, no reasoning, no intellectual quibbling, no rebellion, but a strict, steadfast loyalty of spirit to God, a life of loyalty in heart and intellect to God's Word.

God has much to do with believing men, who have a living, transforming faith in Jesus Christ.

These are God's children. A father loves his children, supplies their needs, hears their cries and answers their requests. A child believes his father, loves him, trusts in him, and asks him for what he needs, believing without doubting that his father will hear his requests. God has everything to do with answering the prayer of His children. Their troubles concern Him, and their prayers awaken Him. Their voice is sweet to Him. He loves to hear them pray, and He is never happier than to answer their prayers.

Prayer is intended for God's ear. It is not man, but God who hears and answers prayer. Prayer covers the whole range of man's need. Hence, " in everything, by prayer and supplication," are " requests to be made known unto God." Prayer includes the entire range of God's ability. " Is anything too hard for God? " Prayer belongs to no favoured segment of man's need, but reaches to and embraces the entire circle of his wants, simply because God is the God of the whole man. God has pledged Himself to supply the needs of the whole man, physical, intellectual and spiritual. " But my God shall supply all your need according to his riches in glory by Christ Jesus." Prayer is the child of grace, and grace is for the whole man, and for every one of the children of men.

VI

PRAYING MEN AT A PREMIUM

" Our Redeemer was in the Garden of Gethsemane. His hour was come. He felt as if He would be strengthened somewhat, if He had two or three disciples near Him. His three chosen disciples were within a stone's-cast of the scene of His agony; but they were all asleep that the Scripture might be fulfilled—' I have trodden the winepress alone, and of the people there was none with Me.' The eight, in the distance, were good and true disciples; but they were only ordinary men, or men with a commonplace call."—ALEXANDER WHYTE.

NO insistence in the Bible is more pressing than the injunction it lays upon men to pray. No exhortation contained therein is more hearty, more solemn, and more stirring. No principle is more strongly inculcated than that " men ought always to pray and not to faint." In view of this enjoinder it is pertinent to inquire as to whether Christian people are praying men and women in anything like body and bulk? Is prayer a fixed course in the schools of the Church? In the Sunday school, the home, the colleges, have we any graduates in the school of prayer? Is the Church producing those who have diplomas from the great university of prayer? This is what God requires, what He commands, and it is those who possess such qualifications that He must have to accom-

plish His purposes and to carry out the work of
His Kingdom on earth.

And it is earnest praying that had need to be
done. Languid praying, without heart or strength,
with neither fire nor tenacity, defeats its own
avowed purpose. The prophet of olden times laments that in a day which needed strenuous praying there was no one who " stirred up himself to
take hold of God." Christ charges us "not to faint"
in our praying. Laxity and indifference are great
hindrances to prayer, both to the practice of praying and the process of receiving; it requires a
brave, strong, fearless and insistent spirit to engage
in successful prayer. Diffuseness, too, interferes
with effectiveness. Too many petitions break ten-
sion and unity, and breed neglect. Prayers should
be specific and urgent. Too many words, like too
much width, breeds shallows and sand-bars. A
single objective which absorbs the whole being and
inflames the entire man, is the properly constrain-
ing force in prayer.

It is easy to see how prayer was a decreed factor
in the dispensations preceding the coming of Jesus,
and how that their leaders had to be men of prayer;
how that God's mightiest revelation of Himself was
a revelation made through prayer. And, finally, how
that Jesus Christ, in His personal ministry, and in
His relation to God, was great and constant in
prayer. His labours and dispensation overflowed
with fullness in proportion to His prayers. The
possibilities of His praying were unlimited and the
possibilities of His ministry were in keeping. The

necessity of His praying was equalled only by the constancy with which He practiced it during His earthly life.

The dispensation of the Holy Spirit is a dispensation of prayer, in a preëminent sense. Here prayer has an essential and vital relation. Without depreciating the possibilities and necessities of prayer in all the preceding dispensations of God in the world it must be declared that it is in this latter dispensation that the engagements and demands of prayer are given their greatest authority, their possibilities rendered unlimited and their necessity insuperable.

These days of ours have sore need of a generation of praying men, a band of men and women through whom God can bring His great and His greatest movements more fully into the world. The Lord our God is not straitened within Himself, but He *is* straitened in us, by reason of our little faith and weak praying. A breed of Christian is greatly needed who will seek tirelessly after God,—who will give Him no rest, day and night, until He hearken to their cry. The times demand praying men who are all athirst for God's glory, who are broad and unselfish in their desires, quenchless for God, who seek Him late and early, and who will give themselves no rest until the whole earth be filled with His glory.

Men and women are needed whose prayers will give to the world the utmost power of God; who will make His promises to blossom with rich and full results. God is waiting to hear us and challenges us to bring Him to do this thing by our praying. He is asking us, to-day, as He did His ancient Israel, to " prove Him now herewith." Behind God's Word is God Himself, and we read: " Thus saith the Lord, the Holy One of Israel, his Maker: Ask of me of things to come and concerning my sons, and concerning the work of my hands, command ye me." As though God places Himself in the hands and at the disposal of His people who pray—as indeed He does.

The dominant element of all praying is faith, that is conspicuous, cardinal and emphatic. Without such faith it is impossible to please God, and equally impossible to pray.

There is a current conception of spiritual duties which tends to separate the pulpit and the pew, as though the pulpit bore the entire burden of spiritual concerns, and while the pew was concerned only with duties that relate to the lower sphere of the secular and worldly. Such a view needs drastic correction. God's cause, its obligations, efforts and successes, lie with equal pressure on pulpit and pew.

But the man in the pew is not taxed with the burden of prayer as he ought to be, and as he *must* be, ere any new visitation of power come to the Church. The Church never will be wholly for God until the pews are filled with praying men. The Church cannot be what God wants it to be until those of its members who are leaders in business, politics, law, and society, are leaders in prayer.

God began His early movements in the world

with men of prayer. He chose such a man to be the father of that race who became His chosen people in the world for hundreds of years, to whom He committed His oracles, and from whom sprang the Promised Messiah. Abraham, a leader of God's cause, was preëminently a praying man. When we consider his conduct and character, we readily see how prayer ruled and swayed this great leader of God's people in the wilderness. "Abraham planted a grove in Beersheba, and called there on the name of the Lord, the everlasting God," and it is an outstanding fact that wherever he pitched his tent and camped for a season, with his household, there he erected the altar of sacrifice and of prayer. His was a personal and a family religion, in which prayer was a prominent and abiding factor.

Prayer is the medium of divine revelation. It is through prayer that God reveals Himself to the spiritual soul to-day, just as in the Old Testament days He made His revelations to the men who prayed. God shows Himself to the man who prays. " God is with thee in all that thou doest." This was the clear conviction of those who would fain make a covenant with Abraham, and the reason for this tribute was the belief commonly held concerning the patriarch that, not only was he a man of prayer, but a man whose prayers God would answer. This is the summary and secret of divine rule in the Church. In all ages God has ruled the Church by prayerful men. When prayer fails, the divine rulership fails. As we have seen, Abraham, the father of the faithful, was a prince and a priest in prayer. He had remarkable influence with God. God stays His vengeance while Abraham prays. His mercy is suspended and conditioned on Abraham's praying. His visitations of wrath are removed by the praying of this ruler in Israel. The movements of God are influenced by the prayers of Abraham, the friend of God. Abraham's righteous prayerfulness permits him to share the secrets of God's counsels, while the knowledge of these secrets draws out and intensifies his praying. With Abraham, the altar of sacrifice is hard by the altar of prayer. With him the altar of prayer sanctifies the altar of sacrifice. To Abimelech God said, " Abraham is a prophet, and he shall pray for thee, and thou shalt live."

Christian people *must* pray for men. On one occasion, Samuel said unto the people, " Moreover as for me, God forbid that I should sin against the Lord in ceasing to pray for you." Fortunate for these sinful people who had rejected God, and desired a human king, that they had in Israel a man of prayer. The royal way to enlarge personal grace is to pray for others. Intercessory prayer is a means of grace to those who exercise it. We enter the richest fields of spiritual growth and gather its priceless riches in the avenues of intercessory prayer. To pray for men is of divine nomination, and represents the highest form of Christian service.

Men must pray, and men must be prayed for. The Christian must pray for all things, of course, but prayers for men are infinitely more important, just as men are infinitely more important than things. So also prayers for men are far more important than prayers for things because men more deeply concern God's will and the work of Jesus Christ than things. Men are to be cared for, sympathized with and prayed for, because sympathy, pity, compassion and care accompany and precede prayer for men, when they are not called out for things.

All this makes praying a real business, not child's play, not a secondary affair, nor a trivial matter but a serious business. The men who have made a success of praying have made a business of praying. It is a process demanding the time, thought, energy and hearts of mankind. Prayer is business for time, business for eternity. It is a man's business to pray, transcending all other business and taking precedence over all other vocations, professions or occupations. Our praying concerns ourselves, all men, their greatest interests, even the salvation of their immortal souls. Praying is a business which takes hold of eternity and the things beyond the grave. It is a business which involves earth and heaven. All worlds are touched and worlds are influenced by prayer. It has to do with God and men, angels and devils.

Jesus was preëminently a leader in prayer, and His praying is an incentive to prayer. How prominently prayer stands out in His life! The leading events of His earthly career are distinctly marked by prayer. The wonderful experience and glory of the Transfiguration was preceded by prayer, and was the result of the praying of our Lord. What words He used as He prayed we know not, nor do we know for what He prayed. But doubtless it was night, and long into its hours the Master prayed. It was while He prayed the darkness fled, and His form was lit with unearthly splendour. Moses and Elijah came to yield to Him not only the palm of law and prophecy, but the palm of praying. None other prayed as did Jesus nor had any such a glorious manifestation of the divine presence or heard so clearly the revealing voice of the Father, " This is my beloved Son; hear ye him." Happy disciples to be with Christ in the school of prayer!

How many of us have failed to come to this glorious Mount of Transfiguration because we were unacquainted with the transfiguring power of prayer! It is the going apart to pray, the long, intense seasons of prayer, in which we engage which makes the face to shine, transfigures the character, makes even dull, earthly garments to glisten with heavenly splendour. But more than this: it is real praying which makes eternal things real, close and tangible, and which brings the glorified visitors and the heavenly visions. Transfigured lives would not be so rare if there were more of this transfigured praying. These heavenly visits would not be so few if there was more of this transfigured praying.

How difficult it appears to be for the Church to understand that the whole scheme of redemption depends upon men of prayer! The work of our Lord, while here on the earth, as well of the Apostle

Paul was, by teaching and example, to develop men of prayer, to whom the future of the Church should be committed. How strange that instead of learning this simple and all important lesson, the modern Church has largely overlooked it! We have need to turn afresh to that wondrous Leader of spiritual Israel, our Lord Jesus Christ, who by example and precept enjoins us to prayer and to the great Apostle to the Gentiles, who by virtue of his praying habits and prayer lessons is a model and an example to God's people in every age and clime.

VII

THE MINISTRY AND PRAYER

" Of course the preacher is above all others distinguished as a man of prayer. He prays as an ordinary Christian, else he were a hypocrite. He prays more than ordinary Christians else he were disqualified for the office he has undertaken. If you as ministers are not very prayerful you are to be pitied. If you become lax in sacred devotion, not only will you need to be pitied but your people also, and the day cometh in which you will be ashamed and confounded. Our seasons of fastings and prayer at the Tabernacle have been high days indeed; never has heaven's gate stood wider; never have our hearts been nearer the central glory."—CHARLES HADDON SPURGEON.

PREACHERS are God's leaders. They are divinely called to their holy office and high purpose and, primarily, are responsible for the condition of the Church. Just as Moses was called of God to lead Israel out of Egypt through the wilderness into the Promised Land, so, also, does God call His ministers to lead His spiritual Israel through this world unto the heavenly land. They are divinely commissioned to leadership, and are by precept and example to teach God's people what God would have them be. Paul's counsel to the young preacher Timothy is in point: " Let no man despise thy youth," he says, " but be thou an example of the believers, in word, conversation, in charity, in spirit, in faith, in purity."

God's ministers shape the Church's character,

and give tone and direction to its life.   The prefacing sentence of the letter to each of the seven churches in Asia reads, " To the angel of the Church," seeming to indicate that the angel—the minister—was in the same state of mind and condition of life as the membership and that these " angels " or ministers were largely responsible for the spiritual condition of things existing in each Church.   The " angel " in each case was the preacher, teacher, or leader.   The first Christians knew full well and felt this responsibility.   In their helplessness, consciously felt, they cried out, "And who is sufficient for things? " as the tremendous responsibility pressed upon their hearts and heads. The only reply to such a question was, " God only."   So they were necessarily compelled to look beyond themselves for help and throw themselves on prayer to secure God.   More and more as they prayed, did they feel their responsibility, and more and more by prayer did they get God's help.   They realized that their sufficiency was of God.

Prayer belongs in a very high and important sense to the ministry.   It takes vigour and elevation of character to administer the prayer-office. Praying prophets have frequently been at a premium in the history of God's people.   In every age the demand has been for leaders in Israel who pray. God's watchmen must always and everywhere be men of prayer.

It ought to be no surprise for ministers to be often found on their knees seeking divine help under the responsibility of their call.   These are the true prophets of the Lord, and these are they who stand as mouthpieces of God to a generation of wicked and worldly-minded men and women. Praying preachers are boldest, the truest and the swiftest ministers of God. They mount up highest and are nearest to Him who has called them. They advance more rapidly and in Christian living are most like God.

In reading the record of the four evangelists, we cannot but be impressed by the supreme effort made by our Lord to rightly instruct the twelve Apostles in the things which would properly qualify them for the tremendous tasks which would be theirs after He had gone back to the bosom of the Father. His solicitude was for the Church that she should have men, holy in life and in heart, and who would know full well from whence came their strength and power in the work of the ministry. A large part of Christ's teaching was addressed to these chosen Apostles, and the training of the twelve occupied much of His thought and consumed much of His time. In all that training, prayer was laid down as a basic principle.

We find the same thing to be true in the life and work of the Apostle Paul. While he addressed himself to the edification of the churches to whom he ministered and wrote, it was in his mind and purpose to rightly instruct and prepare ministers to whom would be committed the interests of God's people. The two epistles to Timothy were addressed to a young preacher, while that to Titus was also written to a young minister. And Paul's design appears to have been to give to each of them such instruction as would be needed rightly to do the work of the ministry to which they had been called by the Spirit of God. Underlying these instructions was the foundation-stone of prayer, since by no means would they be able to " show themselves approved unto God, workmen that needeth not to be ashamed, rightly dividing the word of truth," unless they were men of prayer.

The highest welfare of the Church of God on earth depends largely upon the ministry, and so Almighty God has always been jealous of His watchmen—His preachers. His concern has been for the character of the men who minister at His altars in holy things. They must be men who lean upon Him, who look to Him, and who continually seek Him for wisdom, help and power effectively to do the work of the ministry. And so He has designed men of prayer for the holy office, and has relied upon them successively to perform the tasks He has assigned them.

God's great works are to be done as Christ did them; are to be done, indeed, with increased power received from the ascended and exalted Christ. These works are to be done by prayer. Men must do God's work in God's way, and to God's glory, and prayer is a necessity to its successful accomplishment.

The thing far above all other things in the equipment of the preacher is prayer. Before everything else, he must be a man who makes a specialty of prayer. A prayerless preacher is a misnomer. He has either missed his calling, or has grievously failed God who called him into the ministry. God wants men who are not ignoramuses, who " study to show themselves approved." Preaching the Word is essential; social qualities are not to be underestimated, and education is good; but under and above all else, prayer must be the main plank in the platform of the man who goes forth to preach the unsearchable riches of Christ to a lost and hungry world. The one weak spot in our Church institutions lies just here. Prayer is not regarded as being the primary factor in church life and activity, and other things, good in their places, are made primary. First things need to be put first, and the first thing in the equipment of a minister is prayer.

Our Lord is the pattern for all preachers, and, with Him, prayer was the law of life. By it He lived. It was the inspiration of His toil, the source of His strength, the spring of His joy. With our Lord prayer was no sentimental episode, nor an afterthought, nor a pleasing, diverting prelude, nor an interlude, nor a parade or form. For Jesus, prayer was exacting, all-absorbing, paramount. It was the call of a sweet duty to Him, the satisfying of a restless yearning, the preparation for heavy responsibilities, and the meeting of a vigorous need. This being so, the disciple must be as his Lord, the servant as his Master. As was the Lord Himself, so also must be those whom He has called to be His disciples. Our Lord Jesus Christ chose His twelve Apostles only after He had spent a night in praying; and we may rest assured that He sets the same high value on those He calls to His ministry, in this our own day and time.

No feeble or secondary place was given to prayer in the minstry of Jesus. It comes first—emphatic, conspicuous, controlling. Of prayerful habits, of a prayerful spirit, given to long solitary communion with God, Jesus was above all else, a man of prayer. The crux of His earthly history, in New Testament terminology, is condensed to a single statement, to be found in Hebrews 5: 7:

"Who in the days of his flesh, when he had offered up prayers and supplications with strong crying and tears, unto him that was able to save him from death, and was heard in that he feared."

As was their Lord and Master, whose they are and whom they serve, so let His ministers be. Let Him be their pattern, their example, their leader and teacher. Much reference is made in some quarters about "following Christ," but it is confined to the following of Him in modes and ordinances, as if salvation were wrapped up in the specific way of doing a thing. "The path of prayer Thyself hath trod," is the path along which we are to follow Him, and in no other. Jesus was given as a leader to the people of God, and no leader ever exemplified more the worth and necessity of prayer. Equal in glory with the Father, anointed and sent on His special mission by the Holy Spirit, His incarnate birth, His high commission, His royal anointing,—all these were His but they did not relieve Him from the exacting claims of prayer. Rather did they tend to impose these claims upon Him with greater authority. He did not ask to be excused from the burden of prayer; He gladly accepted it, acknowledged its claims and voluntarily subjected Himself to its demands.

His leadership was preëminent, and His praying was preëminent. Had it not been, His leadership had been neither preëminent nor divine. If, in true leadership, prayer had been dispensable, then certainly Jesus could have dispensed with it. But He did not, nor can any of His followers who desire effectiveness in Christian activity do other than follow their Lord.

While Jesus Christ practiced praying Himself, being personally under the law of prayer, and while His parables and miracles were but exponents of prayer, He laboured directly to teach His disciples the specific art of praying. He said little or nothing about how to preach or what to preach. But He spent His strength and time in teaching men how to speak to God, how to commune with Him, and how to be with Him. He knew full well that he who has learned the craft of talking to God, will be well versed in talking to men. We may turn aside for a moment to observe that this was the secret of the wonderful success of the early Methodist preachers, who were far from being learned men. But with all their limitations, they were men of prayer, and they did great things for God.

All ability to talk to men is measured by the ability with which a preacher can talk to God for men. He " who ploughs not in his closet, will never reap in his pulpit."

The fact must ever be kept in the forefront and emphasized that Jesus Christ trained His disciples to pray. This is the real meaning of that saying, " The Training of the Twelve." It must be kept in mind that Christ taught the world's preachers more about praying than He did about preaching. Prayer was the great factor in the spreading of His Gospel. Prayer conserved and made efficient all other factors. Yet He did not discount preaching when He stressed praying, but rather taught the utter dependence of preaching on prayer.

" The Christian's trade is praying," declared Martin Luther. Every Jewish boy had to learn a trade. Jesus Christ learned two, the trade of a carpenter, and that of praying. The one trade subserved earthly uses; the other served His divine and higher purposes. Jewish custom committed Jesus when a boy to the trade of a carpenter; the law of God bound Him to praying from His earliest years, and remained with Him to the end.

Christ is the Christian's example, and every Christian must pattern after Him. Every preacher must be like his Lord and Master, and must learn the trade of praying. He who learns well the trade of praying masters the secret of the Christian art, and becomes a skilled workman in God's workshop, one who needeth not to be ashamed, a worker together with his Lord and Master.

" Pray without ceasing," is the trumpet call to the preachers of our time. If the preachers will get their thoughts clothed with the atmosphere of prayer, if they will prepare their sermons on their knees, a gracious outpouring of God's Spirit will come upon the earth.

The one indispensable qualification for preaching is the gift of the Holy Spirit, and it was for the bestowal of this indispensable gift that the disciples were charged to tarry in Jerusalem. The absolute necessity there is for receiving this gift if success is to attend the efforts of the ministry, is found in the command the first disciples had to stay in Jerusalem till they received it, and also with the instant and earnest prayerfulness with which they sought it. In obedience to their Lord's command to tarry in that city till they were endued with power from on high, they immediately, after He left them for heaven, entered on securing it by continued and earnest prayer. " These all with one accord, continued steadfastly in prayer, with the women, and Mary the mother of Jesus and with his brethren." To this same thing John refers in his First Epistle. " Ye have an unction from the Holy One," he says. It is this divine unction that preachers of the present day should sincerely desire, pray for, remaining unsatisfied till the blessed gift be richly bestowed.

Another allusion to this same important procedure is made by our Lord shortly after His resurrection, when He said to His disciples: " And ye shall receive power after that the Holy Ghost is come upon you." At the same time Jesus directed the attention of His disciples to the statement of John the Baptist concerning the Spirit, the identical thing for which He had commanded them to tarry in the city of Jerusalem—" power from on high." Alluding to John the Baptist's words Jesus said, " For John indeed baptized with water, but ye shall be baptized with the Holy Ghost not many days hence." Peter at a later date said of our Lord: " God anointed him with the Holy Ghost and with power."

These are the divine statements of the mission and ministry of the Holy Spirit to preachers of that day and the same divine statements apply with equal force to the preachers of *this* day. God's ideal minister is a God-called, divinely anointed, Spirit-touched man, separated unto God's work, set apart from secularities and questionable affairs, baptized from above, marked, sealed and owned by the Spirit, devoted to his Master and His ministry. These are the divinely-appointed requisites for a preacher of the Word; without them, he is inadequate, and inevitably unfruitful.

To-day, there is no dearth of preachers who deliver eloquent sermons on the need and nature of revival, and advance elaborate plans for the spread of the kingdom of God, but the praying preachers are far more rare and the greatest benefactor this age can have is a man who will bring the preachers, the Church and the people back to the practice of real praying. The reformer needed just now is the praying reformer. The leader Israel requires is one who, with clarion voice, will call the ministry back to their knees.

There is considerable talk of the coming revival in the air, but we need to have the vision to see that the revival we need and the only one that can be worth having is one that is born of the Holy Spirit, which brings deep conviction for sin, and regeneration for those who seek God's face. Such a revival comes at the end of a season of real praying, and it is utter folly to talk about or expect a revival without the Holy Spirit operating in His peculiar office, conditioned on much earnest praying. Such a revival will begin in pulpit and pew alike, will be promoted by both preacher and layman working in harmony with God.

The heart is the lexicon of prayer; the life the best commentary on prayer, and the outward bearing its fullest expression. The character is made by prayer; the life is perfected by prayer. And this the ministry needs to learn as thoroughly as the laymen. There is but one rule for both.

So averse was the general body of Christ's disciples to prayer, having so little taste for it, and having so little sympathy with Him in the deep things of prayer, and its mightier struggles, that the Master had to select a circle of three more apt scholars—Peter, James and John—who had more of sympathy, and relish for this divine work, and take them aside that they might learn the lesson of prayer. These men were nearer to Jesus, fuller of sympathy, and more helpful to Him because they were more prayerful.

Blessed, indeed, are those disciples whom Jesus Christ, in this day, calls into a more intimate fellowship with Him, and who, readily responding to the call, are found much on their knees before Him. Distressing, indeed, is the condition of those servants of Jesus who, in their hearts, are averse to the exercise of the ministry of prayer.

All the great eras of our Lord, historical and spiritual, were made or fashioned by His praying. In like manner His plans and great achievements were born in prayer and impregnated by the spirit thereof. As was the Master, so also must His servant be; as his Lord did in the great eras of His life, so should the disciple do when faced by important crises. " To your knees, O Israel! " should be the clarion-call to the ministry of this generation.

The highest form of religious life is attained by prayer. The richest revelations of God—Father, Son, and Spirit—are made, not to the learned, the great or the " noble " of earth, but men of prayer. " For ye see your calling, brethren, that not many wise men after the flesh, not many mighty, not many noble, are called," to whom God makes known the deep things of God, and reveals the higher things of His character, but to the lowly, inquiring, praying ones. And again must it be said, this is as true of preachers as of laymen. It is the spiritual man who prays, and to praying ones God makes His revelations through the Holy Spirit.

Praying preachers have always brought the greater glory to God, have moved His Gospel onward with its greatest, speediest rate and power.

A non-praying preacher and a non-praying Church may flourish outwardly and advance in many aspects of their life. Both preacher and church may become synonyms for success, but unless it rest on a praying basis all success will eventually crumble into deadened life and ultimate decay.

" Ye have not because ye ask not," is the solution of all spiritual weakness both in the personal life and in the pulpit. Either that or it is, " Ye ask and receive not because ye ask amiss." Real praying lies at the foundation of all real success of the ministry in the things of God. The stability, energy and facility with which God's kingdom is established in this world are dependent upon prayer. God has made it so, and so God is anxious for men to pray. Especially is He concerned that His chosen ministers shall be men of prayer, and so gives that wonderful statement in order to encourage His ministers to pray, which is found in Matthew 6: 9:

" But I say unto you, Ask, and it shall be given you; seek, and ye shall find; knock, and it shall be opened unto you. For every one that asketh, receiveth, and he that seeketh, findeth; and to him that knocketh, it shall be opened."

Thus both command and direct promise give accent to His concern that they shall pray. Pause and think on these familiar words. " Ask, and it shall be given you." That itself would seem to be enough to set us all, laymen and preachers, to praying, so direct, simple and unlimited. These words open all the treasures of heaven to us, simply by asking for them.

If we have not studied the prayers of Paul, primarily a preacher to the Gentiles, we can have but a feeble view of the great necessity for prayer, and how much it is worth in the life and the work of a minister of the Gospel. Furthermore, we shall have but a very limited view of the possibilities of the Gospel to enrich and make strong and perfect Christian character, as well as to equip preachers for their high and holy task. Oh, when will we learn the simple yet all important lesson that the one great thing needed in the life of a preacher to help him in his personal life, to keep his soul alive to God, and to give efficacy to the Word preached by him, is real, constant prayer!

Paul with prayer uppermost in his mind, assures the Colossians that " Epaphras is always labouring fervently for you in prayers, that ye may stand complete and perfect in all the will of God." To this high state of grace, " complete in all the will of God," he prays they may come. So prayer was the force which was to bring them to that elevated, vigorous and stable state of heart. This is in line with Paul's teaching to the Ephesians, " And he gave some pastors and teachers, for the perfecting of the saints, for the work of the ministry, for the edifying of the body of Christ," where it is evidently affirmed that the whole work of the ministry is not merely to induce sinners to repent, but it is also the " perfecting of the saints." And so Epaphras " laboured fervently in prayers " for this thing. Certainly he was himself a praying man, in thus so earnestly praying for these early Christians.

The Apostles put out their force in order that Christians should honour God by the purity and consistency of their outward lives. They were to reproduce the character of Jesus Christ. They were to perfect His image in themselves, imbibe His temper and reflect His carriage in all their tempers and conduct. They were to be imitators of God as dear children, to be holy as He was holy. Thus even laymen were to preach by their conduct and character, just as the ministry preached with their mouths.

To elevate the followers of Christ to these exalted heights of Christian experience, they were in every way true in the ministry of God's Word, in the ministry of prayer, in holy consuming zeal, in burning exhortation, in rebuke and reproof. Added to all these, sanctifying all these, invigorating all these, and making all of them salutary, they centered and exercised constantly the force of mightiest praying. "Night and day praying exceedingly," that is, praying out of measure, with intense earnestness, superabundantly, beyond measure, exceeding abundantly.

" Night and day praying exceeding abundantly, that we might see your face, and might perfect that which is lacking in your faith. Now God himself, and our Father, and our Lord Jesus Christ, direct our way unto you.

" And the Lord make you to increase and abound in love one toward another, and toward all men, even as we do toward you; to the end he may establish your hearts unblamable in holiness before God, even our Father, at the coming of our Lord Jesus Christ with all his saints."

It was after this fashion that these Apostles—the first preachers in the early Church—laboured in prayer. And only those who labour after the same fashion are the true successors of these Apostles. This is the true, the Scriptural " apostolical succession," the succession of simple faith, earnest desire for holiness of heart and life, and zealous praying. These are the things to-day which make the ministry strong, faithful and efficient, " workmen who needeth not to be ashamed, rightly dividing the word of truth."

Jesus Christ, God's Leader and Commander of His people, lived and suffered under this law of prayer. All His personal conquests in His life on earth were won by obedience to this law, while the conquests which have been won by His representatives since He ascended to heaven, were gained only when this condition of prayer was heartily and fully met. Christ was under this one prayer condition. His Apostles were under the same prayer condition. His saints are under it, and even His angels are under it. By every token, therefore, preachers are under the same prayer law. Not for one moment are they relieved or excused from obedience to the law of prayer. It is their very life, the source of their power, the secret of their religious experience and communion with God.

Christ could do nothing without prayer. Christ could do all things by prayer. The Apostles were helpless without prayer—and were absolutely dependent upon it for success in defeating their spiritual foes. They could do all things by prayer.

VIII

PRAYERLESSNESS IN THE PULPIT

" Henry Martyn laments that ' want of private devotional reading and shortness of prayer through incessant sermon-making had produced much strangeness between God and his soul.' He judges that he had dedicated too much time to public ministrations and too little to private communion with God. He was much impressed with the need of setting apart times for fasting and to devote times to for solemn prayer. Resulting from this he records ' Was assisted this morning to pray for two hours.' "

—E. M. B.

ALL God's saints came to their sainthood by the way of prayer. The saints could do nothing without prayer. We can go further and say that the angels in heaven can do nothing without prayer, but can do all things by praying. These messengers of the Highest are largely dependent on the prayers of the saints for the sphere and power of their usefulness, which open avenues for angelic usefulness and create missions for them on the earth. And as it is with all the Apostles, saints and angels in heaven, so is it of preachers. " The angels of the churches " can do nothing without prayer which opens doors of usefulness and gives power and point to their words.

How can a preacher preach effectively, make impressions on hearts and minds, and have fruits to his ministry, who does not get his message first-hand from God? How can he deliver a rightful message without having his faith quickened, his vision cleared, and his heart warmed by his closeting with God?

It would be well for all of us, in this connection, to read again Isaiah's vision recorded in the seventh chapter of his prophecy when, as he waited, and confessed and prayed before the throne, the angel touched his lips with a live coal from God's altar:

" Then flew one of the seraphim unto me," he says, " having a live coal in his hand, which he had taken with the tongs from off the altar; and he laid it upon my mouth, and said, Lo, this hath touched thy lips, and thy iniquity is taken away and thy sin is purged."

Oh, the need there is for present-day preachers to have their lips touched with a live coal from the altar of God! This fire is brought to the mouths of those prophets who are of a prayerful spirit, and who wait in the secret place for the appointed angel to bring the living flame. Preachers of the same temper as Isaiah received visits from the angel who brings live coals to touch their lips. Prayer always brings the living flame to unloose tongues, to open doors of utterance, and to open great and effectual doors of doing good. This, above all else, is the great need of the prophets of God.

As far as the abiding interests of religion are concerned, a pulpit without a closet will always be a barren thing. Blessed is the preacher whose pulpit and closet are hard by each other, and who goes from the one into the other. To consecrate no place to prayer, is to make a beggarly showing, not only in praying, but in holy living, for secret prayer and holy living are so closely joined that they can never be dissevered. A preacher or a Christian may live a decent, religious life, without secret prayer, but decency and holiness are two widely different things. And the former is attained only by secret prayer.

A preacher may preach in an official, entertaining and learned way, without prayer, but between this kind of preaching and the sowing of God's precious seed there is distance not easily covered.

We cannot declare too often or too strongly that prayer, involving all of its elements, is the one prime condition of the success of Christ's kingdom, and that all else is secondary and incidental. Prayerful preachers, prayerful men and prayerful women only can press this Gospel with aggressive power. They only can put in it conquering forces. Preachers may be sent out by the thousand, their equipments be ever so complete, but unless they be men skilled in the trade of prayer, trained to its martial and exhaustive exercise, their going will be lacking in power and effectiveness. Moreover, except the men and women who are behind these preachers, who furnish their equipment, are men and women in whose characters prayer has become to be serious labour, their outlay will be a vain and bootless effort.

Prayer should be the inseparable accompaniment of all missionary effort, and must be the one equipment of the missionaries as they go out to their fields of labour, and enter upon their delicate and responsible tasks. Prayer and missions go hand in hand. A prayerless missionary is a failure before he goes out, while he *is* out, and when he returns to his native land. A prayerless board of missions, too, needs to learn the lesson of the necessity of prayer.

Prayer enthrones God as sovereign and elevates Jesus Christ to sit with Him, and had Christian preachers used to its full the power of prayer, long ere this the " kingdoms of this world would have become the kingdom of God and of his Christ." Added to all the missionary addresses, the money raised for missions, to the scores being sent out to needy fields, is prayer. Missions have their root in prayer, must have prayer in all of its plans, and prayer must precede, go with and follow all of its missionaries and labourers.

In the face of all difficulties which face the Church in its great work on earth, and the almost superhuman and complex obstacles in the way of evangelizing the world, God encourages us by His strongest promises: " Call unto me and I will answer thee, and show great and mighty things which thou knowest not." The revelations of God to him who is of a prayerful spirit go far beyond the limits of the praying. God commits Himself to answer the specific prayer, but He does not stop there. He says, " Ask of me things to come concerning my sons, and concerning the work of my hands, command ye me." Think over that remarkable engagement of God to those who pray. " Command ye me." He actually places Himself at the command of praying preachers and a praying Church. And this is a sufficient answer to all doubts, fears and unbelief, and a wonderful inspiration to do God's work in His own way, which means by the way of prayer.

And as if to still fortify the faith of His ministry and of His Church, to hedge about and fortify against any temptation to doubt or discouragement, He declares by the mouth of the great Apostle to the Gentiles, " He is able to do exceeding abundantly above all that ye can ask or think."

It is unquestionably taught that preachers in going forward with their God-appointed tasks, in their prayers, can command God, which is to command His ability, His presence and His power. " Certainly I will be with thee," is the reply to every sincere inquiring minister of God. All of God's called men in the ministry are privileged to stretch their prayers into regions where neither words nor thought can go, and are permitted to expect from Him beyond their praying, and for their praying, God Himself, and then in addition, " great and mighty things which thou knowest not."

Real heart-praying, live-praying, praying by the power of the Spirit, direct, specific, ardent, simple praying—this is the kind of praying which legitimately belongs to the pulpit. This is the kind demanded just now by the men who stand in the pulpit. There is no school in which to learn to pray in public but in the closet. Preachers who have learned to pray in the closet, have mastered the secret of pulpit praying. It is but a short step from secret praying to effectual, live, pulpit praying. Good pulpit praying follows from good secret praying. A closed closet with the preacher makes for cold, spiritless, formal praying in the pulpit. Study how to pray, O preacher, but not by studying the forms of prayer, but by attending the school of prayer on your knees before God. Here is where we learn not only to pray before God, but learn also how to pray in the presence of men. He who has learned the way to the closet has discovered the way to pray when he enters the pulpit.

How easily we become professional and mechanical in the most sacred undertakings! Henry Martyn learned the lesson so hard to learn, that the cultivation and perfection of personal righteousness was the great and prime factor in the preacher's true success. So likewise he that learns the lesson so hard to learn, that live, spiritual, effective pulpit praying is the outgrowth of regular secret praying, has learned his lesson well. Moreover: his work, as a preacher, will depend upon his praying.

The great need of the hour is for good pray-ers in the pulpit as well as good preachers. Just as live, spiritual preaching is the kind which impresses and moves men, so the same kind of pulpit praying moves and impresses God. Not only is the preacher called to preach well, but also he must be called to pray well. Not that he is called to pray after the fashion of the Pharisees, who love to stand in public and pray that they may be seen and heard of men. The right sort of pulpit praying is far removed from Pharisaical praying, as far distant as light is from darkness, as great as heat is from cold, as life is from death.

Where are we? What are we doing? Preaching is the very loftiest work possible for a man to do. And praying goes hand-in-hand with preaching. It is a mighty, a lofty work. Preaching is a life-giving work, sowing the seeds of eternal life. Oh, may we do it well, do it after God's order, do it successfully! May we do it divinely well, so that when the end comes, the solemn close of earthly probation, we may hear from the Great Judge of all the earth, " Well done, good and faithful servant, enter thou into the joy of thy Lord."

When we consider this great question of preaching, we are led to exclaim, " With what reverence, simplicity and sincerity ought it to be done! " What truth in the inward parts is demanded in order that it be done acceptably to God and with profit to men! How real, true and loyal those who practise it ought to be! How great the need to pray as Christ prayed, with strong cryings, and tears, with godly fear! Oh, may we as preachers do the real thing of preaching, with no sham, with no mere form of words, with no dull, cold, professional utterances, but give ourselves to prayerful preaching and prayerful praying! Preaching which gives life is born of praying which gives life. Preaching and praying always go together, like Siamese twins, and can never be separated without death to one or the other, or death to both.

This is not the time for kid-glove methods nor sugar-coated preaching. This is no time for playing the gentleman as a preacher nor for putting on the garb of the scholar in the pulpit, if we propose to disciple all nations, destroy idolatry, crush the rugged and defiant forces of Mohammedanism, and overcome and destroy the tremendous forces of evil now opposing the kingdom of God in this world. Brave men, true men, praying men—afraid of nothing but God, are the kind needed just now. There will be no smiting the forces of evil which now hold the world in thraldom, no lifting of the degraded hordes of paganism, to light and eternal life, by any but praying men. All others are merely playing at religion, make-believe soldiers, with no armour and no ammunition, who are absolutely helpless in the face of a wicked and gainsaying world. None but soldiers and bond servants of Jesus Christ can possibly do this tremendous work. "Endure hardness as a good soldier of Jesus Christ," cries the great Apostle. This is no time to think of self, to consult with dignity, to confer with flesh and blood, to think of ease, or to shrink from hardship, grief and loss. This is the time for toil, suffering, and self-denial. We must lose all for Christ in order to gain all for Christ. Men are needed in the pulpit, as well as in the pew, who are "bold to take up, firm to sustain, the consecrated cross." Here is the sort of preachers God wants.

And this sort are born of much praying. For no man is sufficient for these things who is a prayerless preacher. Praying preachers alone can meet the demand and will be equal to the emergency.

The Gospel of Jesus has neither relish nor life in it when spoken by prayerless lips or handled by prayerless hands. Without prayer the doctrines of Christ degenerate into dead orthodoxy. Preaching them without the aid of the Spirit of God, who comes into the preacher's messages only by prayer, is nothing more than mere lecturing, with no life, no grip, no force in the preaching. It amounts to nothing more than live rationalism or sickly sentimentalism. " But we will give ourselves continually to prayer and to the ministry of the Word," was the settled and declared purpose of the apostolic ministry. The kingdom of God waits on prayer, and prayer puts wings on the Gospel and power into it. By prayer it moves forward with conquering force and rapid advance.

If prayer be left out of account, the preacher rises to no higher level than the lecturer, the politician or the secular teacher. That which distinguishes him from all other public speakers is the fact of prayer. And as prayer deals with God, this means that the preacher has God with him, while other speakers do not need God with them to make their public messages effective. The preacher above everything else is a spiritual man, a man of the Spirit, who deals with spiritual things. And this implies that he has to do with God in His pulpit work in a high and holy sense. This can be said of no other public speaker. And so prayer must necessarily go with the preacher and his preaching. Pure intellectuality is the only qualification for other public speakers. Spirituality which is born of prayer belongs to the preacher.

In the Sermon on the Mount Jesus Christ often speaks of prayer. It stands out prominently in His utterances on that occasion. The lesson of prayer which He taught was one of hallowing God's name, of pushing God's kingdom. We are to long for the coming of the kingdom of God. It is to be longed for, and must be first in our intercourse with God. God's will must have its royal way in the hearts and wills of those who pray. The point of urgency is made by our Lord that men are to pray in earnest, by asking, seeking, knocking, in order to hallow God's name, bring His will to pass, and to forward His kingdom among men.

And let it be kept in mind that while this prayer-lesson has to do with all men, it has a peculiar application to the ministry, for it was the twelve would-be preachers who made the request of our Lord Jesus Christ, " Lord, teach us to pray, as John also taught his disciples." So that primarily these words were spoken first to twelve men just entering upon their work as ministers. Jesus was talking as Luke records it, to preachers. So He speaks to the preachers of this day. How He pressed these twelve men into the ministry of prayer! The present-day ministry needs the same lesson to be taught them, and needs the same urgency pressing them to prayer as their habit of life.

Notwithstanding all he may claim for himself, nor how many good things may be put down to his credit, a prayerless preacher will never learn well God's truth, which He is called upon to declare with all fidelity and plainness of speech. Blind and blinding still will he be if he lives a prayerless life. A prayerless ministry cannot know God's truth, and not knowing it, cannot teach it to ignorant men. He who teaches us the path of prayer, must first of all walk in the same path. A preacher cannot teach what he does not know. A blind leader of the blind will be the preacher who is a stranger to prayer. Prayer opens the preacher's eyes, and keeps them open to the evil of sin, the peril of it, and the penalty it incurs. A blind leader leading the blind will be the vocation of him who is prayerless in his own life.

The best and the greatest offering which the Church and the ministry can make to God is an offering of prayer. If the preachers of the twentieth century will learn well the lesson of prayer, and use it fully in all its exhaustless efficiency, the millennium will come to its noon ere the century closes.

The Bible preacher prays. He is filled with the Holy Spirit, filled with God's Word, and is filled with faith. He has faith in God, faith in God's only begotten Son, his personal Saviour, and he has implicit faith in God's Word. He cannot do otherwise than pray. He cannot be other than a man of prayer. The breadth of his life and the pulsations of his heart are prayer. The Bible preacher lives by prayer, loves by prayer, and preaches by prayer. His bended knees in the place of secret prayer advertise what kind of preacher he is.

Preachers may lose faith in God, in Jesus Christ as their personal and present Saviour, become devoid of the peace of God and let the joy of salvation go out of their hearts, and yet be unconscious of it. How needful for the preacher to be continually examining himself, and inquiring into his personal relations to God and into his religious state! The preachers, like the philosophers of old, may defer to a system, and earnestly contend for it after they have lost all faith in its great facts. Men may in the pulpit with hearts of unbelief, minister at the altars of the Church, while alien to the most sacred and vital principles of the Gospel.

It is a comparatively easy task for preachers to become so absorbed in the material and external affairs of the Church as to lose sight of their own souls, forget the necessity of prayer so needful to keep their own souls alive to God, and lose the inward sweetness of a Christian experience.

The prayer which makes much of our preaching must itself be made much of. The character of our praying will determine the character of our preaching. Serious praying will give serious weight to preaching. Prayer makes preaching strong, gives it unction and makes it stick. In every ministry, weighty for good, prayer has always been a serious business prophetic of good.

It cannot be said with too much emphasis, the preacher must be preëminently a man of prayer.

He must learn to pray, and he must have such an estimate of prayer and its great worth that he feels he cannot afford to omit it from the catalogue of his private duties. His heart must be attuned to prayer, while he himself touches the highest note of prayer. In the school of prayer only can the heart learn to preach. No gifts, no learning, no brain-force, can atone for the failure to pray. No earnestness, no diligence, no study, no amount of social service, will supply its lack. Talking to men for God may be a great thing, and may be very commendable. But talking to God for men, is far more valuable and commendable.

The power of Bible preaching lies not simply or solely in superlative devotion to God's Word, and jealous passion for God's truth. All these are essential, valuable, helpful. But above all these things, there must be the sense of the divine presence, and the consciousness of the divine power of God's Spirit on the preacher and in him. He must have an anointing, an empowering, a sealing of the Holy Spirit, for the great work of preaching, making him akin to God's voice, and giving him the energy of God's right hand, so that this Bible preacher can say, " Thy words were found, and I did eat them; and thy word was unto me the joy and rejoicing of my heart. For I am called by thy name, O Lord of hosts."

IX

PRAYER-EQUIPMENT FOR PREACHERS

" Go back! Back to that upper room; back to your knees;
back to searching of heart and habit, thought and life; back to
pleading, praying, waiting, till the Spirit of the Lord floods the
soul with light, and you are endued with power from on high.
Then go forth in the power of Pentecost, and the Christ-life
shall be lived, and the works of Christ shall be done. You shall
open blind eyes, cleanse foul hearts, break men's fetters, and save
men's souls. In the power of the indwelling Spirit, miracles
become the commonplace of daily living."—SAMUEL CHADWICK.

ALMOST the last words uttered by our Lord
before His ascension to heaven, were
those addressed to the eleven disciples,
words which, really, were spoken to, and having directly to do with, preachers, words which indicate
very clearly the needed fitness which these men
must have to preach the Gospel, beginning at
Jerusalem: " But tarry ye in the city of Jerusalem,"
says Jesus, " till ye be endued with power from
on high."

Two things are very clearly set forth in these
urgent directions. First, the power of the Holy
Ghost for which they must tarry. This was to be
received after their conversion, an indispensable
requisite, equipping them for the great task set
before them. Secondly, the " promise of the Fa-

ther," this "power from on high," would come to them after they had waited in earnest, continuous prayer. A reference to Acts 1: 14 will reveal that these same men, with the women, "continued with one accord in prayer and supplication," and so continued until the Day of Pentecost, when the power from on high descended upon them.

This "power from on high," as important to those early preachers as it is to present-day preachers, was not the force of a mighty intellect, holding in its grasp great truths, flooding them with light, and forming them into verbal shapeliness and beauty. Nor was it the acquisition of great learning, or the result of an address, faultless and complete by rule of rhetoric. None of these things. Nor was this spiritual power held then, nor is it held now, in the keeping of any earthly sources of power. The effect and energy of all human forces are essentially different in source and character, and do not at all result from this "power from on high." The transmission of such power is directly from God, a bestowal, in rich measure, of the force and energy which pertains only to God, and which is transmitted to His messengers only in answer to a longing, wrestling attiude of his soul before his Master, conscious of his own impotency and seeking the omnipotency of the Lord he serves, in order more fully to understand the given Word and to preach the same to his fellow-men.

The "power from on high" may be found in combination with all sources of human power, but is not to be confounded with them, is not dependent upon them, and must never be superseded by them. Whatever of human gift, talent or force a preacher may possess it is not to be made paramount, or even conspicuous. It must be hidden, lost, overshadowed by this "power from on high." The forces of intellect and culture may all be present, but without this inward, heaven-given power, all spiritual effort is vain and unsuccessful. Even when lacking the other equipment but having this "power from on high," a preacher cannot but succeed. It is the one essential, all-important vital force which a messenger of God must possess to give wings to his message, to put life into his preaching, and to enable him to speak the Word with acceptance and power.

A word is necessary here. Distinctions need to be kept in mind. We must think clearly upon this question. "Power from on high" means "the unction of the Holy One" resting on and abiding in the preacher. This is not so much a power which bears witness to a man being the child of God as it is a preparation for delivering the Word to others. Unction must be distinguished from pathos. Pathos may exist in a sermon while unction is entirely absent. So also, may unction be present and pathos absent. Both may exist together; but they are not to be confused, nor be made to appear to be the same thing. Pathos promotes emotion, tender feeling, sometimes tears. Quite often it results from the relation of an affecting incident, or when the tender side is peculiarly appealed to. But pathos is neither the direct nor indirect result of the Holy Spirit resting upon the preacher as he preaches.

But unction is. Here we are given the evidence of the workings of an undefinable agency in the preacher, which results directly from the presence of this "power from on high," deep, conscious, life-giving and carrying, giving power and point to the preached Word. It is the element in a sermon which arouses, stirs, convicts and moves the souls of sinners and saints. This is what the preacher requires, the great equipment for which he should wait and pray. This "unction of the Holy One" delivers from dryness, saves from superficiality, and gives authority to preaching. It is the one quality which distinguishes the preacher of the Gospel from other men who speak in public; it is that which makes a sermon unique, unlike the deliverance of any other public speaker.

Prayer is the language of a man burdened with a sense of need. It is the voice of the beggar, conscious of his poverty, asking of another the things he needs. It is not only the language of lack, but of *felt lack*, of lack consciously realized. "Blessed are the poor in spirit," means not only that the fact of poverty of spirit brings the blessing, but also that poverty of spirit is realized, known and acknowledged. Prayer is the language of those who need something—something which they, themselves, cannot supply but which God has promised them, and for which they ask. In the end, poor praying and prayerlessness amount to the same thing, for poor praying proceeds from a lack of the sense of need, while prayerlessness has its origin in the same soil. Not to pray is not only to declare there is nothing needed, but to admit to a non-realization of that need. This is what aggravates the sin of prayerlessness. It represents an attempt at instituting an independence of God, a self-sufficient ruling of God out of the life. It is a declaration made to God that we do not need Him, and hence do not pray to Him.

This is the state in which the Holy Spirit, in His messages to the Seven Churches in Asia, found the Laodicean Church and " the Laodicean state " has come to stand for one in which God is ruled out, expelled from the life, put out of the pulpit. The entire condemnation of this Church is summed up in one expression: " Because thou sayest, I have need of nothing," the most alarming state into which a person, or church or preacher can come. Trusting in its riches, in its social position, in things outward and material, the Church at Laodicea omitted God, leaving Him out of their church plans and church work, and declared, by their acts and by their omission of prayer, " I have need of nothing."

No wonder the self-satisfied declaration brought forth its sentence of punishment—" Because thou art lukewarm, and neither cold nor hot, I will spue thee out of my mouth." The idea conveyed is that such a backslidden state of heart is as repulsive to God as an emetic is to the human stomach, and as the stomach expels that which is objectionable, so Almighty God threatens to " spue out of His

mouth " these people who were in such a religious
condition so repulsive to Him. All of it was traceable to a prayerless state of heart, for no one can
read this word of the Spirit to this Laodicean
Church and not see that the very core of their sin
was prayerlessness. How could a Church, given
to prayer, openly and vauntingly declare, " I have
need of nothing," in the face of the Spirit's assertion that it needed everything, " Thou knowest not
that thou art wretched, and poor, and miserable,
and blind, and naked "?   In addition to their sin
of self-sufficiency and of independence of God, the
Laodiceans were spiritually blind. Oh, what dull-
ness of sight, what blindness of soul! These people were prayerless, and knew not the import of
such prayerlessness.   They lacked everything
which goes to make up spiritual life, and force, and
self-denying piety, and vainly supposed themselves
to need nothing but material wealth, thus making
temporal possessions a substitute for spiritual
wealth, leaving God entirely out of their activities,
relying upon human and material resources to do
the work only possible to the divine and supernatural, and secured alone by prayer.

Nor let it be forgotten that this letter (in common with the other six letters) was primarily addressed to the preacher in charge of the church. All
this strengthens the impression that the " angel of
the church " himself was in this lukewarm state. He
himself was living a prayerless life, relying upon
things other than God, practically saying, " I have
need of nothing." For these words are the natural

expression of the spirit of him who does not pray, who does not care for God, and who does not feel the need of Him in his life, in his work and in his preaching. Furthermore, the words of the Spirit seem to indicate that the " angel of the church " at Laodicea was indirectly responsible for this sad condition into which the Laodicean Church had fallen.

May not this sort of a church be found in modern times? Is it not likely that we could discover some preachers of modern times who fall under a similar condemnation to that passed upon the " angel of the church " of Laodicea?

Preachers of the present age excel those of the past in many, possibly in all, human elements of success. They are well abreast of the age in learning, research, and intellectual vigour. But these things neither insure " power from on high " nor guarantee a live, thriving religious experience, or righteous life. These purely human gifts do not bring with them an insight into the deep things of God, or strong faith in the Scriptures, or an intense loyalty to God's divine revelation.

The presence of these earthly talents even in the most commanding and impressive form, and richest measure do not in the least abate the necessity for the added endowment of the Holy Spirit. Herein lies the great danger menacing the pulpit of to-day. All around us we see a tendency to substitute human gifts and worldly attainments for that supernatural, inward power which comes from on high in answer to earnest prayer.

In many instances modern preaching seems to fail in the very thing which should create and distinguish true preaching, which is essential to its being, and which alone can make of it a divine and powerfully aggressive agency. It lacks, in short, " the power from on high " which alone can make it a living thing. It fails to become the channel through which God's saving power can be made to appeal to men's consciences and hearts.

Quite often, modern preaching fails at this vital point, for lack of exercising a potent influence which disturbs men in their sleep of security, and awakens them to a sense of need and of peril. There is a growing need of an appeal which will quicken and arouse the conscience from its ignoble stupor and give it a sense of wrong-doing and a corresponding sense of repentance. There is need of a message which searches into the secret places of man's being, dividing, as it were, the joints and the marrow, and laying bare the mysterious depths before himself and his God. Much of our present-day preaching is lacking in that quality which infuses new blood into the heart and veins of faith, that arms it with courage and skill for the battle with the powers of darkness, and secures it a victory over the forces of the world.

Such high and noble ends can never be accomplished by human qualifications, nor can these great results be secured by a pulpit clothed only with the human elements of power, however gracious, comfortable, and helpful they may be. The Holy Spirit is needed. He alone can equip the ministry for its difficult and responsible work in and out of the pulpit. Oh, that the present-day ministry may come to see that its one great need is an enduement of "power from on high," and that this one need can be secured only by the use of God's appointed means of grace—the ministry of prayer.

Prayer is needed by the preacher in order that his personal relations with God may be maintained and that because there is no difference between him and any other kind of a man in so far as his personal salvation is concerned. This he must work out "with fear and trembling," just as all other men must do. Thus prayer is of vast importance to the preacher in order that he may possess a growing religious experience, and be enabled to live such a life that his character and conduct will back up his preaching and give force to his message.

A man *must* have prayer in his pulpit work, for no minister can preach effectively without prayer. He also has use for prayer in praying for others. Paul was a notable example of a preacher who constantly prayed for those to whom he ministered.

But we come, now, to another sphere of prayer, that of the people praying for the preacher. " Brethren, pray for us." This is the cry which Paul set in motion, and which has been the cry of spiritually minded preachers—those who know God and who know that value of prayer—in all succeeding ages. No condition of success or the reverse of it must abate the cry. No degree of culture, no abundance of talents, must cause that cry to cease. The learned preacher, as well as the unlearned, has equal need to call out to the people they serve, " Withal, praying also for us." Such a cry voices the felt need of a preacher's heart who feels the need there is for sympathies of a people to be in harmony with its minister. It is but the expression of the inner soul of a preacher who feels his insufficiency for the tremendous responsibilities of the pulpit, who realizes his weakness and his need of the divine unction, and who throws himself upon the prayers of his congregation, and calls out to them, " Praying always with all prayer and supplication, in the Spirit, and for me, that utterance may be given me." It is the cry of deep felt want in the heart of the preacher who feels he must have this prayer made specifically for him that he may do his work in God's own way.

When this request to a people to pray for the preacher is cold, formal and official, it freezes instead of fructifies. To be ignorant of the necessity for the cry, is to be ignorant of the sources of spiritual success. To fail to stress the cry, and to fail to have responses to it, is to sap the sources of spiritual life. Preachers must sound out the cry to the Church of God. Saints everywhere and of every kind, and of every faith speedily respond and pray for the preacher. The imperative need of the work demands it. " Pray for us," is the natural cry of the hearts of God's called men—faithful preachers of the Word.

Saintly praying in the early Church helped

apostolic preaching mightily, and rescued apostolic men from many dire straits. It can do the same thing to-day. It can open doors for apostolic labours, and apostolic lips to utter bravely and truly the Gospel message. Apostolic movements wait their ordering from prayer, and avenues long closed are opened to apostolic entrance by and through the power of prayer. The messenger receives his message and is schooled as to how to carry and deliver the message by prayer. The forerunner of the Gospel, and that which prepares the way, is prayer; not only by the praying of the messenger himself, but by the praying of the Church of God.

Writing along this line in his Second Epistle to the Thessalonians, Paul is first general in his request and says, " Brethren, pray for us." Then he becomes more minute and particular:

" Finally, brethren, pray for us," he goes on, " that the word of the Lord may have free course and be glorified, even as it is with you. And that we may be delivered from unreasonable and wicked men; for all men have not faith."

The Revised Version has for " free course " the word " run." " The Word " means doctrine, and the idea conveyed is that this doctrine of the Gospel is rapidly propagated, a metaphor taken from the running of a race, and is an exhortation to exert one's self, to strive hard, to expend strength. Thus the prayer for the spread of the Gospel gives the same energy to the Word of the Lord, as the greatest outlay of strength gives success to the racer. Prayer in the pew gives the preached Word energy, facility, and success. Preaching without the backing of mighty praying is as limp and worthless an effort as can be imagined. Prayerlessness in the pew is a serious hindrance to the running of the Word of the Lord.

The preaching of the Word of the Lord fails to run and be glorified from many causes. The difficulty may lie with the preacher himself, should his outward conduct be out of harmony with the rule of the Scriptures and his own profession. The Word *lived* must be in accord with the Word *delivered;* the *life* must be in harmony with the *sermon*. The preacher's spirit and behaviour *out* of the pulpit must run parallel with the Word of the Lord spoken *in* the pulpit. Otherwise, a man is an obstacle to the success of his own message.

Again, the Word of the Lord may fail to run, may be seriously encumbered and crippled by the inconsistent lives of those who are the hearers thereof. Bad living in the pew will seriously cripple the Word of the Lord, as attempts to run on its appointed course. Unrighteous lives among the laity heavily weights down the Word of the Lord and hampers the work of the ministry. Yet prayer will remove this burden which seriously handicaps the preached Word. It will tend to do this in a direct way, or in an indirect manner. For just as you set laymen to praying, for the preacher or even for themselves, it awakens conscience, stirs the heart, and tends to correct evil ways and to promote good living. No man will pray long and continue in sin. Praying breaks up bad living, while bad living breaks down prayer. Praying goes into bankruptcy when a man goes to sinning. To obey the cry of the preacher, " Brethren, pray for us," sets men to doing that which will induce right living in them, and will tend to break them away from sin. So it comes about that it is worth no little to get the laity to pray for the ministry. Prayer helps the preacher, is an aid to the sermon, assists the hearer and promotes right living in the pew.

Prayer also moves him who prays for the preacher and for the Word of the Lord, to use all his influence to remove any hindrance to that Word which he may see, and which lies in his power to remove.

But prayer reaches the preacher directly. God hears the praying of a church for its minister. Prayer for the preached Word is a direct aid to it. Prayer for the preacher gives wings to the Gospel, as well as feet. Prayer makes the Word of the Lord go forward strongly and rapidly. It takes the shackles off of the message, and gives it a chance to run straight to the hearts of sinners and saints, alike. It opens the way, clears the track, furnishes a free course. The failure of many a preacher may be found just here. He was hampered, hindered, crippled by a prayerless church. Non-praying officials stood in the way of the Word preached, and became veritable stumbling blocks in the way of the Word, definitely preventing its reaching the hearts of the unsaved.

Unbelief and prayerlessness go together. It is written of our Lord in Matthew's Gospel that when He entered into His own country, " he did not many mighty works there because of their unbelief." Mark puts it a little differently, but giving out the same idea: "And he could there do no mighty work, save that he laid his hands upon a few sick folks and healed them. And he marveled because of their unbelief." Unquestionably the unbelief of that people hindered our Lord in His gracious work and tied His hands. And if that be true, it requires no undue straining of the Scriptures when we say that the unbelief and prayerlessness of a church can tie the hands of its preacher, and prevent him from doing many great works in the salvation of souls and in edifying saints. Prayerlessness, therefore, as it concerns the preacher is a very serious matter. If it exists in the preacher himself, then he ties his own hands and makes the Word as preached by him ineffective and void. If prayerless men be found in the pew, then it hurts the preacher, robs him of an invaluable help, and interferes seriously with the success of his work. How great the need of a praying church to help on the preaching of the Word of the Lord! Both pew and pulpit are jointly concerned in this preaching business. It is a copartnership. The two go hand in hand. One must help the other, one can hinder the other. Both must work in perfect accord or serious damage will result, and God's plan concerning the preacher and the preached Word be defeated.

X

THE PREACHER'S CRY—" PRAY FOR US! "

" That the true apostolic preacher must have the prayers of others—good people to give to his ministry its full quota of success, Paul is a preëminent example. He asks, he covets, he pleads in an impassionate way for the help of all God's saints. He knew that in the spiritual realm as elsewhere, in union there is strength; that the consecration and aggregation of faith, desire, and prayer increased the volume of spiritual force until it became overwhelming and irresistible in its power. Units of prayer combined, like drops of water, make an ocean that defies resistance."—E. M. B.

HOW far does praying for the preacher help preaching? It helps him personally and officially. It helps him to maintain a righteous life, it helps him in preparing his message, and it helps the Word preached by him to run to its appointed goal, unhindered and unhampered.

A praying church creates a spiritual atmosphere most favourable to preaching. What preacher knowing anything of the real work of preaching doubts the veracity of this statement? The spirit of prayer in a congregation begets an atmosphere surcharged with the Spirit of the Highest, removes obstacles and gives the Word of the Lord right of way. The very attitude of such a congregation constitutes an environment most encouraging and favourable to preaching. It renders preaching an easy task; it enables the Word to run quickly and without friction, helped on by the warmth of souls engaged in prayer.

Men in the pew given to praying for the preacher, are like the poles which hold up the wires along which the electric current runs. They are not the power, neither are they the specific agents in making the Word of the Lord effective. But they hold up the wires, along which the divine power runs to the hearts of men. They give liberty to the preacher, exemption from being straitened, and keep him from " getting in the brush." They make conditions favourable for the preaching of the Gospel. Preachers, not a few, who know God, have had large experience and are aware of the truth of these statements. Yet how hard have they found it to preach in some places! This was because they had no " door of utterance," and were hampered in their delivery, there appearing no response whatever to their appeals. On the other hand, at other times, thought flowed easily, words came freely, and there was no failure in utterance. The preacher " had liberty," as the old men used to declare.

The preaching of the Word to a prayerless congregation falls at the very feet of the preacher. It has no traveling force; it stops because the atmosphere is cold, unsympathetic, unfavourable to its running to the hearts of men and women. Nothing is there to help it along. Just as some prayers never go above the head of him who prays, so the preaching of some preachers goes no farther than the front of the pulpit from which it is delivered. It takes prayer in the pulpit and prayer in the pew to make preaching arresting, life-giving and soul-saving.

The Word of God is inseparably linked with prayer. The two are conjoined, twins from birth, and twins by life. The Apostles found themselves absorbed by the sacred and pressing duty of distributing the alms of the Church, till time was not left for them to pray. They directed that other men should be appointed to discharge this task, that they might be the better able to give themselves continually to prayer and to the ministry of the Word.

So it might likewise be said that prayer for the preacher by the church is also inseparably joined to preaching. A praying church is an invaluable help to the faithful preacher. The Word of the Lord runs in such a church, " and is glorified " in the saving of sinners, in the reclamation of backsliders, and in the sanctifying of believers. Paul connects the Word of God closely in prayer in writing to Timothy:

" For every creature of God is good," he says, " and nothing to be refused, if it be received with thanksgiving. For it is sanctified by the Word of God and prayer."

And so the Word of the Lord is dependent for its rapid spread and for its full, and most glorious success in prayer.

Paul indicates that prayer transmutes the ills which come to the preacher: " For I know that this shall turn to my salvation through your prayer, and the supply of the Spirit of Jesus Christ." It was " through their prayer " he declares these benefits would come to him. And so it is " through the prayer of a church " that the pastor will be the beneficiary of large spiritual things.

In the latter part of the Epistle to the Hebrews, we have Paul's request for prayer for himself addressed to the Hebrew Christians, basing his request on the grave and eternal responsibilities of the office of a preacher:

" Obey them that have the rule over you," he says, " and submit yourselves; for they watch for your souls as they that must give account, that they may do it with joy, and not with grief; for that is unprofitable for you. Pray for us; for we trust we have a good conscience in all things willing to live honestly."

How little does the Church understand the fearful responsibility attaching to the office and work of the ministry! " For they watch for your souls as they that must give account." God's appointed watchmen, to warn when danger is nigh; God's messengers sent to rebuke, reprove and exhort with all long-suffering; ordained as shepherds to protect the sheep against devouring wolves. How responsible is their position! And they are to give account to God for their work, and are to face a day of reckoning. How much do such men need the prayers of those to whom they minister! And who should be more ready to do this praying than God's people, His own Church, those presumably who are in heart sympathy with the minister and his all-important work, divine in its origin.

Among the last messages of Jesus to His disciples are those found in the fourteenth, fifteenth and sixteenth chapters of John's Gospel. In the fourteenth, as well as in the others, are some very specific teachings about prayer, designed for their help and encouragement in their future work. We must never lose sight of the fact that these last discourses of Jesus Christ were given to disciples *alone*, away from the busy crowds, and seem primarily intended for them in their public ministry. In reality, they were words spoken to preachers, for these eleven men were to be the first preachers of the new dispensation.

With this thought in mind, we are able to see the tremendous importance given to prayer by our Lord, and the high place He gave it in the life-work of preachers, both in this day and in that day.

First our Lord proposes that He will pray for these disciples, that the Father might send them another Comforter, even the Spirit of truth, whom the world could not receive. He preceded this statement by a direct command to them to pray, to pray for anything, with the assurance that they would receive what they asked for.

If, therefore, there was value in their own praying, and it was of great worth that our Lord should intercede for them, then of course it would be worth while that the people to whom they would minister should also pray for them. It is no wonder then that the Apostle Paul should take the key from our Lord, and several times break out with the urgent exhortation, " Pray for us."

True praying done by the laymen helps in many ways, but in one particular way. It helps very materially the preacher to be brave and true. Read Paul's request to the Ephesians:

" Praying always with all prayer and supplication," he says, " in the Spirit, and watching thereunto with all perseverance, and supplication for all saints; and for me, that utterance may be given unto me, that I may open my mouth boldly, to make known the mystery of the gospel; for which I am an ambassador in bonds, that therein I may speak as I ought to speak."

How much of the boldness and loyalty of Paul was dependent upon the prayers of the Church, or rather how much he was helped at these two points, we may not know. But unquestionably there must have come to him through the prayers of the Christians at Ephesus, Colossæ and Thessalonica, much aid in preaching the Word, of which he would have been deprived had these churches not have prayed for him. And in like manner, in modern times, has the gift of ready and effective utterance in the preacher been bestowed upon a preacher through the prayers of a praying church.

The Apostle Paul did not desire to fall short of

that most important quality in a preacher of the Gospel, namely, boldness. He was no coward, or time-server, or man-pleaser, but he needed prayer, in order that he might not, through any kind of timidity, fail to declare the whole truth of God, or through fear of men, declare it in an apologetic, hesitating way. He desired to remove himself as far as possible from an attitude of this kind. His constant desire and effort was to declare the Gospel with consecrated boldness and with freedom. "That I may open my mouth boldly, to make known the mystery of the Gospel, that I may speak boldly, as I ought to speak," seemed to be his great desire, and it would appear that, at times, he was really afraid that he might exhibit cowardice, or be affected by the fear of the face of man.

This is a day that has urgent need of men after the mould of the great Apostle—men of courage, brave and true, who are swayed not by the fear of men, or reduced to silence or apology by the dread of consequences. And one way to secure them is for the pew to engage in earnest prayer for the preachers.

In Paul's word to the Ephesian elders given when on his way to Jerusalem, Paul exculpates himself from the charge of blood-guiltiness, in that he had not failed to declare the whole counsel of God to them. To his Philippian brethren, also, he says, that through their prayers, he would prove to be neither ashamed nor afraid.

Nothing, perhaps, can be more detrimental to the advancement of the kingdom of God among men than a timid, or doubtful statement of revealed truth. The man who states only the half of what he believes, stands side by side with the man who fully declares what he only half believes. No coward can preach the Gospel, and declare the whole counsel of God. To do that, a man must be in the battle-attitude not from passion, but by reason of deep conviction, strong conscience and full-orbed courage. Faith is in the custody of a gallant heart while timidity surrenders, always, to a brave spirit. Paul prayed, and prevailed on others to pray that he might be a man of resolute courage, brave enough to do everything but sin. The result of this mutual praying is that history has no finer instance of courage in a minister of Jesus Christ than that displayed in the life of the Apostle Paul. He stands in the premier position as a fearless, uncompromising, God-fearing preacher of the Gospel of his Lord.

God seems to have taken great pains with His prophets of old time to save them from fear while delivering His messages to mankind. He sought in every way to safeguard His spokesmen from the fear of man, and by means of command, reasoning and encouragement sought to render them fearless and true to their high calling. One of the besetting temptations of a preacher is the " fear " of the face of man. Unfortunately, not a few surrender to this fear, and either remain silent at times when they should be boldly eloquent, or temper with smooth words the stern mandate it is theirs to deliver. " The fear of man bringeth a snare."

With this sore temptation Satan often besets the preacher of the Word and few there be who have not felt the force of this temptation. It is the duty of ministers of the Gospel to face this temptation to fear the face of man with resolute courage and to steel themselves against it, and, if need be, trample it under foot. To this important end, the preacher should be prayed for by his church. He needs deliverance from fear, and prayer is the agency whereby it can be driven away and freedom from the bondage of fear given to his soul.

We have a striking picture of the preacher's need of prayer, and of what a people's prayers can do for him in the seventeenth chapter of the Book of Exodus. Israel and Amalek were in battle, and the contest was severe and close. Moses stood on top of the hill with his rod lifted up in his hands, the symbol of power and victory. As long as Moses held up the rod, Israel prevailed, but when he let down his hand with the rod, Amalek prevailed. While the contest was in the balance, Aaron and Hur came to the rescue, and when Moses' hands were heavy, these two men " stayed up his hands, . . . until the going down of the sun. And Joshua discomfited Amalek and his people."

By common consent, this incident in the history of ancient Israel has been recognized as a striking illustration of how a people may sustain their preacher by prayer, and of how victory comes when the people pray for their preacher.

Some of the Lord's very best men in Old Testament times had to be encouraged against fear by

Almighty God.   Moses himself was not free from
the fear which harasses and compromises a leader.
God told him to go to Pharaoh, in these words:
" Come now therefore, and I will send thee unto
Pharaoh, that thou mayst bring forth my people,
the children of Israel, out of Egypt."   But Moses,
largely through fear, began to offer objections and
excuses for not going, until God became angry with
him, and said, finally, that He would send Aaron
with Moses to do the talking, as long as Moses insisted that he " was slow of speech and of slow
tongue."   But the fact was, Moses was afraid of
the face of Pharaoh, and it took God some time to
circumvent his fears and nerve him to face the
Egyptian monarch and deliver God's message to
him.

And Joshua, too, the successor of Moses, and a
man seemingly courageous, must needs be fortified
by God against fear, lest he shrink from duty, and
be reduced to discouragement and timidity.   " Be
strong and of good courage," God commanded him.
" Have I not commanded thee?   Be not afraid,
neither be thou dismayed, for the Lord thy God is
with thee whithersoever thou goest."

As good and true a man as Jeremiah was sorely
tempted to fear and had to be warned and strengthened lest he prove false to his charge.   When God
ordained him a prophet unto the nations, Jeremiah
began to excuse himself on the ground that he could
not speak, being but a child in that regard.   So the
Lord had to safeguard him from the temptation of
fear, that he might not prove faithless: " Thou

therefore, gird up thy loins, and arise, and speak unto them," God said to His servant, " all that I command thee; be not dismayed at their faces, lest I confound thee before them."

Since these great men of old time were so beset with this temptation, and disposed to shrink from duty we need not be surprised that preachers of our own day are to be found in similar case. The devil is the same in all ages; nor has human nature undergone any change. How needful, then, that we pray for the leaders of our Israel especially that they may receive the gift of boldness, and speak the Word of God with courage.

This was one reason why Paul insisted so vigorously that the brethren pray for him, so that a door of utterance might be given him, and that he might be delivered from the fear of man, and blessed with holy boldness in preaching the Word.

The challenge and demand of the world in our own day is that Christianity be made practical; that its precepts be expressed in practice, and brought down from the realm of the ideal to the levels of every-day life. This can be done only by praying men, who being much in sympathy with their ministers will not cease to bear them up in their prayers before God.

A preacher of the Gospel cannot meet the demands made upon him, alone, any more than the vine can bear grapes without branches. The men who sit in the pews are to be the fruit-bearing ones. They are to translate the " ideal " of the pulpit into the " real " of daily life and action. But they will not do it, they cannot do it, if they be not devoted to God and much given to prayer. Devotion to God and devotion to prayer are one and the same thing.

XI

MODERN EXAMPLES OF PRAYER

"When the dragon-fly rends his husk and harnesses himself, in a clean plate of sapphire mail, his is a pilgrimage of one or two sunny days over the fields and pastures wet with dew, yet nothing can exceed the marvelous beauty in which he is decked. No flowers on earth have a richer blue than the pure colour of his cuirass. So is it in the high spiritual sphere. The most complete spiritual loveliness may be obtained in the shortest time, and the stripling may die a hundred years old, in character and grace."—HISTORY OF DAVID BRAINERD.

GOD has not confined Himself to Bible days in showing what can be done through prayer. In modern times, also, He is seen to be the same prayer-hearing God as aforetime. Even in these latter days He has not left Himself without witness. Religious biography and Church history, alike, furnish us with many noble examples and striking illustrations of prayer, its necessity, its worth and its fruits, all tending to the encouragement of the faith of God's saints and all urging them on to more and better praying. God has not confined Himself to Old and New Testament times in employing praying men as His agents in furthering His cause on earth, and He has placed Himself under obligation to answer their prayers just as much as He did the saints of old. A selection from these praying saints of modern times will show us how they valued prayer, what it meant to them, and what it meant to God.

Take for example, the instance of Samuel Rutherford, the Scottish preacher, exiled to the north of Scotland, forbidden to preach, and banished from his home and pastoral charge. Rutherford lived between 1600 and 1661. He was a member of the Westminster Assembly, Principal of New College, and Rector of St. Andrews' University. He is said to have been one of the most moving and affectionate preachers of his time, or, perhaps, in any age of the Church. Men said of him, " He is always praying," and concerning his and his wife's praying, one wrote: " He who had heard either pray or speak, might have learned to bemoan his ignorance. Oh, how many times have I been convinced by observing them of the evil of insincerity before God and unsavouriness in discourse! He so prayed for his people that he himself says, ' There I wrestled with the Angel and prevailed.' "

He was ordered to appear before Parliament to answer the charge of high treason, although a man of scholarly attainments and rare genius. At times he was depressed and gloomy; especially was this the case when he was first banished and silenced from preaching, for there were many murmurings and charges against him. But his losses and crosses were so sanctified that Christ became more and more to him. Marvelous are the statements of his estimate of Christ. This devoted man of prayer wrote many letters during his exile to preachers, to state officers, to lords temporal and spiritual, to honourable and holy men, to honourable and holy women, all breathing an intense devotion to Christ, and all born of a life of great devotion to prayer.

Ardour and panting after God have been characteristics of great souls in all ages of the Church and Samuel Rutherford was a striking example of this fact. He was a living example of the truth that he who prays always, will be enveloped in devotion and joined to Christ in bonds of holy union.

Then there was Henry Martyn, scholar, saint, missionary, and apostle to India. Martyn was born February 18, 1781, and sailed for India August 31, 1805. He died at Tokai, Persia, October 16, 1812. Here is part of what he said about himself while a missionary:

" What a knowledge of man and acquaintance with the Scriptures, and what communion with God and study of my own heart ought to prepare me for the awful work of a messenger from God on business of the soul."

Said one of this consecrated missionary:

" Oh, to be able to emulate his excellencies, his elevation of piety, his diligence, his superiority to the world, his love for souls, his anxiety to improve all occasions to do souls good, his insight into the mystery of Christ, and his heavenly temper! These are the secrets of the wonderful impression he made in India."

It is interesting and profitable to note some of the things which Martyn records in his diary. Here is an example:

" The ways of wisdom appear more sweet and reasonable than ever," he says, " and the world more insipid and vexatious. The chief thing I mourn over is my want of power, and lack of fervour in secret prayer, especially when attempting to plead for the heathen. Warmth does not increase within me in proportion to my light."

If Henry Martyn, so devoted, ardent and prayerful, lamented his lack of power and want of fervour in prayer, how ought our cold and feeble praying abase us in the very dust? Alas, how rare are such praying men in the Church of our own day!

Again we quote a record from his diary. He had been quite ill, but had recovered and was filled with thankfulness because it had pleased God to restore him to life and health again.

" Not that I have yet recovered my former strength," he says, " but I consider myself sufficiently restored to prosecute my journey. My daily prayer is that my late chastisement may have its intended effect, and make me, all the rest of my days, more humble and less self-confident.

" Self-confidence has often led me down fearful lengths, and would, without God's gracious interference, prove my endless perdition. I seem to be made to feel this evil of my heart more than any other at this time.

In prayer, or when I write or converse on the subject, Christ appears to me my life and my strength; but at other times I am thoughtless and bold, as if I had all life and strength in myself. Such neglects on our part are a diminution of our joys."

Among the last entries in this consecrated missionary's journal we find the following:

" I sat in the orchard and thought, with sweet comfort and peace, of my God, in solitude, my Company, my Friend, my Comforter. Oh, when shall time give place to eternity! "

Note the words, " in solitude,"—away from the busy haunts of men, in a lonely place, like his Lord, he went out to meditate and pray.

Brief as this summary is, it suffices to show how fully and faithfully Henry Martyn exercised his ministry of prayer. The following may well serve to end our portrayal of him:

" By daily weighing the Scriptures, with prayer, he waxed riper and riper in his ministry. Prayer and the Holy Scriptures were those wells of salvation out of which he drew daily the living water for his thirsty immortal soul. Truly may it be said of him, he prayed always with all prayer and supplication, in the Spirit, and watched thereunto with all perseverance."

David Brainerd, the missionary to the Indians, is a remarkable example of a praying man of God. Robert Hale thus speaks of him:

" Such invincible patience and self-denial; such profound humility, exquisite prudence, indefatigable industry; such devotedness to God, or rather such absorption of the whole soul in zeal for the divine glory and the salvation of men, is scarcely to be paralleled since the age of the Apostles. Such was the intense ardour of his mind that it seems to have diffused the spirit of a martyr over the common incidents of his life."

Dr. A. J. Gordon speaks thus of Brainerd:

" In passing through Northampton, Mass., I went into the old cemetery, swept off the snow that lay on the top of the slab, and I read these simple words:
" ' Sacred to the memory of David Brainerd, the faithful and devoted missionary to the Susquehanna, Delaware and Stockbridge Indians of America, who died in this town, October 8th, 1717.'
" That was all there was on the slab. Now that great man did his greatest work by prayer. He was in the depths of those forests alone, unable to speak the language of the Indians, but he spent whole days literally in prayer. What was he praying for? He knew he could not reach these savages, for he did not understand their language. If he wanted to speak at all, he must find somebody who could vaguely interpret his thought. Therefore he knew that anything he could do must be absolutely dependent upon God. So he spent whole days in praying, simply that the power of the Holy Ghost might come upon him so unmistakably that these people would not be able to stand before him.
" What was his answer? Once he preached through a drunken interpreter, a man so intoxicated that he could hardly stand up. This was the best he could do.

Yet scores were converted through that sermon. We can account for it only that it was the tremendous power of God behind him.

"Now this man prayed in secret in the forest. A little while afterward, William Carey read his life, and by its impulse he went to India. Payson read it as a young man, over twenty years old, and he said that he had never been so impressed by anything in his life as by the story of Brainerd. Murray McCheyne read it, and he likewise was impressed by it.

"But all I care is simply to enforce this thought, that the hidden life, a life whose days are spent in communion with God, in trying to reach the source of power, is the life that moves the world. Those living such lives may be soon forgotten. There may be no one to speak a eulogy over them when they are dead. The great world may take no account of them. But by and by, the great moving current of their lives will begin to tell, as in the case of this young man, who died at about thirty years of age. The missionary spirit of this nineteenth century is more due to the prayers and consecration of this one man than to any other one.

"So I say. And yet that most remarkable thing is that Jonathan Edwards, who watched over him all those months while he was slowly dying of consumption, should also say: 'I praise God that it was in His Providence that he should die in my house, that I might hear his prayers, and that I might witness his consecration, and that I might be inspired by his example.'

"When Jonathan Edwards wrote that great appeal to Christendom to unite in prayer for the conversion of the world, which has been the trumpet call of modern missions, undoubtedly it was inspired by this dying missionary."

To David Brainerd's spirit, John Wesley bore this testimony:

" I preached and afterward made a collection for the Indian schools in America. A large sum of money is now collected. But will money convert heathens? Find preachers of David Brainerd's spirit, and nothing can stand before them. But without this, what will gold or silver do? No more than lead or iron."

Some selections from Brainerd's diary will be of value as showing what manner of man he was:

" My soul felt a pleasing yet painful concern," he writes, " lest I should spend some moments without God. Oh, may I always live to God! In the evening I was visited by some friends, and spent the time in prayer, and such conversation as tended to edification. It was a comfortable season to my soul. I felt an ardent desire to spend every moment with God. God is unspeakably gracious to me continually. In time past, He has given me inexpressible sweetness in the performance of duty. Frequently my soul has enjoyed much of God, but has been ready to say, ' Lord, it is good to be here; ' and so indulge sloth while I have lived on the sweetness of my feelings. But of late God has been pleased to keep my soul hungry almost continually, so that I have been filled with a kind of pleasing pain. When I really enjoy God, I feel my desires of Him the more insatiable, and my thirstings after holiness the more unquenchable.

" Oh, that I may feel this continual hunger, and not be retarded, but rather animated by every cluster from Canaan, to reach forward in the narrow way, for the full enjoyment and possession of the heavenly inheritance! Oh, may I never loiter in my heavenly journey!

"It seems as if such an unholy wretch as I never could arrive at that blessedness, to be holy as God is holy. At noon I longed for sanctification and conformity to God. Oh, that is the one thing, the all!

"Toward night enjoyed much sweetness in secret prayer, so that my soul longed for an arrival in the heavenly country, the blessed paradise of God."

If inquiry be made as to the secret of David Brainerd's heavenly spirit, his deep consecration and exalted spiritual state, the answer will be found in the last sentence quoted above. He was given to *much secret prayer*, and was so close to God in his life and spirit that prayer brought forth much sweetness to his inner soul.

We have cited the foregoing cases as illustrative of the great fundamental fact that God's great servants are men devoted to the ministry of prayer; that they are God's agents on earth who serve Him in this way, and who carry on His work by this holy means.

Louis Harms was born in Hanover, in 1809, and then came a time when he was powerfully convicted of sin. Said he, "I have never known what fear was. But when I came to the knowledge of my sins, I quaked before the wrath of God, so that my limbs trembled." He was mightily converted to God by reading the Bible. Rationalism, a dead orthodoxy, and worldliness, held the mutitudes round Hermansburgh, his native town. His father, a Lutheran minister, dying, he became his successor.

He began with all the energy of his soul to work for Christ, and to develop a church of a pure, strong type. The fruit was soon evident. There was a quickening on every hand, attendance at public services increased, reverence for the Bible grew, conversation on sacred things revived, while infidelity, worldliness and dead orthodoxy vanished like a passing cloud. Harms proclaimed a conscious and present Christ, the Comforter, in the full energy of His mission, the revival of apostolic piety and power. The entire neighbourhood became regular attendants at church, the Sabbath was restored to its sanctity, and hallowed with strict devotion, family altars were erected in the homes, and when the noon bell sounded, every head was bowed in prayer. In a very short time the whole aspect of the country was entirely changed. The revival in Hermansburgh was essentially a prayer revival, brought about by prayer and yielding fruits of prayer in a rich and an abundant ingathering.

William Carvosso, an old-time Methodist class-leader, was one of the best examples which modern times has afforded of what was probably the religious life of Christians in the apostolic age. He was a prayer-leader, a class-leader, a steward and a trustee, but never aspired to be a preacher. Yet a preacher he was of the very first quality, and a master in the art and science of soul-saving. He was a singular instance of a man learning the sim-

plest rudiments late in life. He had up to the age
of sixty-five years never written a single sentence,
yet he wrote letters which would make volumes,
and a book which was regarded as a spiritual
classic in the great world-wide Methodist Church.

Not a page nor a letter, it is believed, was ever
written by him on any other subject but religion.
Here are some of his brief utterances which give us
an insight into his religious character. " I want to
be more like Jesus." " My soul thirsteth for Thee,
O God." " I see nothing will do, O God, but being
continually filled with Thy presence and glory."

This was the continual out-crying of his inner
soul, and this was the strong inward impulse which
moved the outward man. At one time we hear
him exclaiming, " Glory to God! This is a morning without a cloud." Cloudless days were native
to his sunny religion and his gladsome spirit.
Continual prayer and turning all conversation
toward Christ in every company and in every
home, was the inexorable law he followed, until he
was gathered home.

On the anniversary of his spiritual birth when
he was born again, in great joyousness of spirit he
calls it to mind, and breaks forth: " Blessed be Thy
name, O God! The last has been the best of the
whole. I may say with Bunyan, ' I have got into
that land where the sun shines night and day.' I
thank Thee, O my God, for this heaven, this element of love and joy, in which my soul now lives."

Here is a sample of Carvosso's spiritual experiences, of which he had many:

" I have sometimes had seasons of remarkable visitation from the presence of the Lord," he says. " I well remember one night when in bed being so filled, so overpowered with the glory of God, that had there been a thousand suns shining at noonday, the brightness of that divine glory would have eclipsed the whole. I was constrained to shout aloud for joy. It was the overwhelming power of saving grace. Now it was that I again received the impress of the seal and the earnest of the Spirit in my heart. Beholding as in a glass the glory of the Lord I was changed into the same image from glory to glory by the Spirit of the Lord. Language fails in giving but a faint description of what I there experienced. I can never forget it in time nor to all eternity.

" Many years before I was sealed by the Spirit in a somewhat similar manner. While walking out one day, I was drawn to turn aside on the public road, and under the canopy of the skies, I was moved to kneel down to pray. I had not long been praying with God before I was so visited from Him that I was overpowered by the divine glory, and I shouted till I could be heard at a distance. It was a weight of glory that I seemed incapable of bearing in the body, and therefore I cried out, perhaps unwisely, Lord, stay Thy hand. In this glorious baptism these words came to my heart with indescribable power: ' I have sealed thee unto the day of redemption.'

" Oh, I long to be filled more with God! Lord, stir me up more in earnest. I want to be more like Jesus. I see that nothing will do but being continually filled with the divine presence and glory. I know all that Thou hast is mine, but I want to feel a close union. Lord, increase my faith."

Such was William Carvosso—a man whose life was impregnated with the spirit of prayer, who lived on his knees, so to speak, and who belonged to that company of praying saints which has blessed the earth.

Jonathan Edwards must be placed among the praying saints—one whom God mightily used through the instrumentality of prayer. As in the instance of the great New Englander, purity of heart should be ingrained in the very foundation areas of every man who is a true leader of his fellows and a minister of the Gospel of Christ and a constant practicer in the holy office of prayer. A sample of the utterances of this mighty man of God is here given in the shape of a resolution which he formed, and wrote down:

" Resolved," he says, " to exercise myself in this all my life long, viz., with the greatest openness to declare my ways to God, and to lay my soul open to God—all my sins, temptations, difficulties, sorrows, fears, hopes, desires, and everything and every circumstance."

We are not surprised, therefore, that the result of such fervid and honest praying was to lead him to record in his diary:

" It was my continual strife day and night, and my constant inquiry how I should be more holy, and live more holily. The heaven I desired was a heaven of holiness. I went on with my eager pursuit after more holiness and conformity to Christ."

The character and work of Jonathan Edwards were exemplifications of the great truth that the ministry of prayer is the efficient agency in every truly God-ordered work and life. He himself gives some particulars about his life when a boy. He might well be called the " Isaiah of the Christian dispensation." There was united in him great mental powers, ardent piety, and devotion to study, unequalled save by his devotion to God. Here is what he says about himself:

" When a boy I used to pray five times a day in secret, and to spend much time in religious conversation with other boys. I used to meet with them to pray together. So it is God's will through His wonderful grace, that the prayers of His saints should be one great and principal means of carrying on the designs of Christ's kingdom in the world. Pray much for the ministers and the Church of God."

The great powers of Edwards' mind and heart were exercised to procure an agreed union in extraordinary prayer of God's people everywhere. His life, efforts and his character are an exemplification of his statement.

" The heaven I desire," he says, " is a heaven spent with God; an eternity spent in the presence of divine love, and in holy communion with Christ."

At another time he said:

" The soul of a true Christian appears like a little

white flower in the spring of the year, low and humble on the ground, opening its bosom to receive the pleasant beams of the sun's glory, rejoicing as it were in a calm rapture, diffusing around a sweet fragrance, standing peacefully and lovingly in the midst of other flowers."

Again he writes:

" Once as I rode out in the woods for my health, having alighted from my horse in a retired place, as my manner has been to walk for divine contemplation and prayer, I had a view, that for me was extraordinary, of the glory of the Son of God as Mediator between God and man, and of His wonderful, great, full, pure, and sweet grace and love, and His meek and gentle condescension. This grace that seemed so calm and sweet, appeared also great above the heavens. The person of Christ appeared ineffably excellent with an excellency great enough to swallow up all thought and conception, which continued, as near as I can judge, about an hour. It kept me the greater part of the time in a flood of tears and weeping aloud. I felt an ardency of soul to be, what I know not otherwise how to express, emptied and annihilated, to lie in the dust; to be full of Christ alone, to love Him with my whole heart."

As it was with Jonathan Edwards, so it is with all great intercessors. They come into that holy and elect condition of mind and heart by a thorough self-dedication to God, by periods of God's revelation to them, making distinct marked eras in their spiritual history, eras never to be forgotten, in which faith mounts up with wings as eagles, and has given it a new and fuller vision of God, a stronger grasp of faith, a sweeter, clearer vision of all things heavenly, and eternal, and a blessed intimacy with, and access to, God.

XII

MODERN EXAMPLES OF PRAYER
(*Continued*)

"Edward Bounds did not merely pray well that he might write well about prayer. He prayed for long years upon subjects to which easy-going Christians rarely give a thought. He prayed for objects which men of less faith are ready to call impossible. Yet from these continued, solitary prayer-vigils, year by year there arose a gift of prayer-teaching equaled by few men. He wrote transcendently about prayer because he was transcendent in its practice."—C. L. CHILTON, JR.

LADY MAXWELL was contemporary with John Wesley, and a fruit of Methodism in its earlier phases. She was a woman of refinement, of culture and of deep piety. Separating herself entirely from the world, she sought and found the deepest religious experience, and was a woman fully set apart to God. Her life was one of prayer, of complete consecration to God, living to bless others. She was noted for her systematic habits of life, which entered into and controlled her religion. Her time was economized and ordered for God. She arose at four o'clock in the morning, and attended preaching at five o'clock. After breakfast she held a family service. Then, from eleven to twelve o'clock she observed a season of intercessory prayer. The rest of the day was given to reading, visiting and acts of benevolence.

Her evenings were spent in reading. At night, before retiring, religious services were held for the family and sometimes in praising God for His mercies.

Rarely has God been served with more intelligence, or out of a richer experience, a nobler ardour, a richer nobility of soul. Strongly, spiritually and ardently attached to Wesley's doctrine of entire dedication, she sought it with persistency, and a never flagging zeal. She obtained it by faith and prayer, and illustrated it in a life as holy and as perfect as is given mortals to reach. If this great feature of Wesley's teaching had, to-day, models and teachers possessed of the profound spiritual understanding and experience as had Fletcher of Madeley and Lady Maxwell of Edinburgh, it would not have been so misunderstood, but would have commended itself to the good and pure everywhere by holy lives, if not by its verbiage.

Lady Maxwell's diary yields some rich counsel for secret prayer, holy experience, and consecrated living. One of the entries runs as follows:

" Of late I feel painfully convinced that I do not pray enough. Lord, give me the spirit of prayer and of supplication. Oh, what a cause of thankfulness is it that we have a gracious God to whom to go on all occasions! Use and enjoy this privilege and you can never be miserable. Who gives thanks for this royal privilege? It puts God in everything, His wisdom, power, control and safety. Oh, what an unspeakable privilege is prayer! Let us give thanks for it. I do not prove all the power of prayer that I wish."

Thus we see that the remedy for non-praying is *praying*. The cure for little praying is more praying. Praying can procure all things necessary for our good.

With this excellent woman praying embraced all things and included everything. To one of her most intimate friends she writes:

" I wish I could provide you with a proper maid, but it is a difficult matter. You have my prayers for it, and if I hear of one I will let you know."

So small a matter as the want of a housemaid for a friend was with her an event not too small to take to God in prayer.

In the same letter, she tells her friend that she wants " more faith. Cry mightily for it, and stir up the gift of God that is in you." '

Whether the need was a small secular thing as a servant, or a great spiritual grace, prayer was the means to attain that end and supply that want. " There is nothing," she writes to a dear correspondent, " so hurtful to the nervous system as anxiety. It preys upon the vitals and weakens the whole frame, and what is more than all, it grieves the Holy Spirit." Her remedy, again, for a common evil, was prayer.

How prayer disburdens us of care by bringing God in to relieve and possess and hold!

" Be careful for nothing," says the Apostle, " but in everything by prayer and supplication, with thanksgiv-

ing, let your requests be made known unto God. And
the peace of God which passeth all understanding shall
keep your hearts and minds through Christ Jesus."

The figure is that of a beleagured and distressed
garrison, unable to protect the fort from the enemies which assault it, into which strong reinforce-
ments are poured. Into the heart oppressed, dis-
tracted and discouraged, true prayer brings God,
who holds it in perfect peace and in perfect safety.
This Lady Maxwell fully understood theoretically,
but which was better, experimentally.

Christ Jesus is the only cure for undue care and
over anxiety of soul, and we secure God, His presence and His peace by prayer. Care is so natural
and so strong, that none but God can eject it. It
takes God, the presence and personality of God
Himself, to oust the care and to enthrone quietness
and peace. When Christ comes in with His peace,
all tormenting fears are gone, trepidation and har-
rowing anxieties capitulate to the reign of peace,
and all disturbing elements depart. Anxious
thought and care assault the soul, and feebleness,
faintness and cowardice are within. Prayer rein-
forces with God's peace, and the heart is kept by
Him. " Thou wilt keep him in perfect peace whose
mind is stayed on Thee." All now is safety, quietness and assurance. " The work of righteousness
is peace, and the effect of righteousness, quietness
and assurance forever."

But to ensure this great peace, prayer must pass
into strenuous, insistent, personal supplication, and

thanksgiving must bloom into full flower. Our exposed condition of heart must be brought to the knowledge of God, by prayer and supplication, with thanksgiving. The peace of God will keep the heart and thoughts, fixed and fearless. Peace, deep, exhaustless, wide, flowing like a river, will come in.

Referring again to Lady Maxwell, we hear her saying:

" God is daily teaching me more simplicity of spirit, and makes me willing to receive all as His unmerited gift, and to call on Him for everything I need, as I need it, and He supplies my wants according to existing needs. But I have certainly felt more of it this last eighteen months than in former periods. I wish to pray without ceasing. I see the necessity of praying always, and not fainting."

Again we hear her declaring: " I wish to be much in prayer. I greatly need it. The prayer of faith shuts or opens heaven. Come, Lord, and turn my captivity." If we felt the need of prayer as this saintly woman did, we could bear her company in her saintly ascension. Prayer truly " shuts or opens heaven." Oh, for a quality of faith that would test to the uttermost the power of prayer!

Lady Maxwell utters a great truth when she says:

" When God is at work either among a people, or in the heart of an individual, the adversary of souls is peculiarly at work also. A belief of the former should prevent discouragement, and a fear of the latter should stir us up to much prayer. Oh, the power of faithful prayer! I live by prayer! May you prove its sovereign efficacy in every difficult case."

We find a record among Lady Maxwell's writings which shows us that in prayer and meditation she obtained enlarged views of the full salvation of God, and what is thus discovered, faith goes out after, and according to its strength are its returns.

" I daily feel the need of the precious blood of sprinkling," she says, " and dwell continually under its influence, and most sensibly feel its sovereign efficacy. It is by momentary faith in this blood alone that I am saved from sin. Prayer is my chief employ."

If this last statement " prayer, the chief employ " had ever been true of God's people, this world would have been by this time quite another world, and God's glory, instead of being dim, and shadowy, and only in spots, would now shine with universal and unrivaled effulgence and power.

Here is another record of her ardent and faithful praying: " Lately, I have been favoured with a more ardent spirit of praying than almost ever formerly."

We need to study these words—" favoured with a more ardent spirit of praying "—for they are pregnant words. The spirit of prayer, the ardent spirit of prayer and its increase, and the more ardent spirit of prayer—all these are of God. They are given in answer to prayer. The spirit of prayer and the more ardent spirit are the result of ardent, importunate secret prayer.

At another time, Lady Maxwell declared that secret prayer was the means whereby she derived the greatest spiritual benefit.

" I do indeed prove it to be an especial privilege," she says. " I could not live without it, though I do not always find comfort in it. I still ardently desire an enlarged sphere of usefulness, and find it comfortable to embrace the opportunities afforded me."

An " enlarged sphere of usefulness " is certainly a proper theme of intense prayer, but that prayer must ever be accompanied with an improvement of the opportunities afforded by the present.

Many pages might be filled with extracts from Lady Maxwell's diary as to the vital importance of, and the nature of the ministry of prayer, but we must forbear. For many years she was in ardent supplication for an enlargement of her sphere of usefulness, but all these years of ardent praying may be condensed into one statement:

" My whole soul has been thirsting after a larger sphere of action," she says, " agreeably to the promises of a faithful God. For these few last weeks I have been led to plead earnestly for more holiness. Lord, give me both, that I may praise Thee."

These two things, for which this godly woman prayed, must go together. They are one, and not to be separated. The desire for a larger field of work without the accompanying desire for an increase of consecration, is perilous, and may be supremely selfish, the offspring of spiritual pride.

John Fletcher, also a contemporary of John Wesley, was intimately associated with the founder of Methodism. He was a scholar of courtesy and refinement, a strong, original thinker, eloquent in simplicity and truth. That which qualified him as a spiritual leader was his exceedingly great faith in God, his nearness to God and his perfect assurance of dear unquestioned relationship to his Lord. Fletcher had profound convictions concerning the truth of God, a deep and perpetual communion with his Lord and Saviour, and was profound and humble in his knowledge of God and Christian experience. He was a man of deep spiritual insight into the things of God, and his thorough earnestness, his truth, and his consecration, marked him as a man of God, well equipped by all these things for a leader in Israel.

Unceasing prayer was the sign and secret of Fletcher's sainthood, its power and influence. His whole life was one of prayer. So intently was his mind fixed on God, that he sometimes said, " I would not rise from my seat without lifting up my heart to God." A friend relates the fact that whenever they met, his first salute was, " Do I meet you praying? " If they were talking on theology, in the midst of it he would break off abruptly and say, " Where are our hearts now? " If the misconduct of any person who was absent was mentioned, he would say, " Let us pray for him."

The very walls of his room—so it was said—were stained by the breath of his prayers. Spiritually, Madeley was a dreary, desolate desert when he went to live there, but it was so revolutionized by his prayers that it bloomed and blossomed like the garden of the Lord. A friend of his thus writes of Fletcher:

" Many of us have at times gone with him aside, and there we would continue for two or three hours, wrestling like Jacob for the blessing, praying one after another. And I have seen him on these occasions so filled with the love of God that he could contain no more, but would cry out, ' O my God, withhold Thy hand or the vessel will burst! ' His whole life was a life of prayer."

John Foster, a man of exalted piety and deep devotion to God, while on his dying bed, thus spoke concerning prayer when about to depart this life:

" Pray without ceasing has been the sentence repeating itself in my silent thoughts, and I am sure that it will be, it must be, my practice till the last conscious hour of my life. O why was it not my practice throughout that long, indolent, inanimate half century past! I often think mournfully of the difference it would have made in me. Now there remains so little time for a mere genuine, effective spiritual life."

The Reformation of the fifteenth century owes its

origin to prayer. In all his life-work, begun, continued and ended, Martin Luther was instant in prayer. The secret of his extraordinary activity is found in this statement: " I have so much work to do that I cannot get along without giving three hours daily of my best time to prayer." Another of his sayings was, " It takes meditation and prayer to make a divine," while his every day motto was, " He that has prayed well, has studied well."

At another time he thus confessed his lack: " I was short and superficial in prayer this morning," he says. How often is this the case with us! Let it be remembered that the source of decline in religion and the proof of decline in a Christian life is found just here, in " short and superficial praying." Such praying betokens and secures strangeness with God.

William Wilberforce once said of himself: " I have been keeping too late hours, and hence have had but a hurried half hour to myself. I am lean and cold and hard. I had better allow more time, say two hours, or an hour-and-a-half, daily to religious exercises."

He must be much skilled and habituated to long praying whose short prayers are not superficial Short prayers make shallow lives. Longer praying would work like magic in many a decayed spiritual life. A holy life would not be so difficult and rare a thing if our praying was not so brief, cold and superficial.

George Muller, that remarkable man of such simple yet strong faith in God, a man of prayer and

Bible reading, founder and promoter of the noted orphanage in England, which cared for hundreds of orphan children, conducted the institution solely by faith and prayer. He never asked a man for anything, but simply trusted in the Providence of God, and it is a notorious fact that never did the inmates of the home lack any good thing. From his paper he always excluded money matters, and financial difficulties found no place in it. Nor would he mention the sums which had been given him, nor the names of those who made contributions. He never spoke of his wants to others nor asked a donation. The story of his life and the history of this orphanage read like a chapter from the Scriptures. The secret of his success was found in this simple statement made by him: " I went to my God and prayed diligently, and received what I needed." That was the simple course which he pursued. There was nothing he insisted on with greater earnestness than that, be the expenses what they might be, let them increase ever so suddenly, he must not beg for anything. There was nothing in which he took more delight and showed more earnestness in telling than that he had prayed for every want which ever came to him in his great work. His was a work of continuous and most importunate praying, and he always confidently claimed that God had guided him throughout it all. A stronger proof of a divine providence, and of the power of simple faith and of answered prayer, cannot be found in Church history or religious biography.

In writing to a friend at one time, John Wesley helps, urges and prays, as we will see from the following from his own pen: " Have you received a gleam of light from above, a spark of faith? If you have, let it not go! Hold fast .by His grace that earnest of your inheritance. Come just as you are, and come boldly to the throne of grace. You need not delay. Even now the bowels of Jesus yearn over you. What have you to do with to-morrow? I love you to-day. And how much more does He love you?

" ' He pities still His wandering sheep,
    And longs to bring you to His fold.'

" To-day hear His voice, the voice of Him that speaks as never man spake."

The seekings of Madame Guyon after God were sincere, and her yearnings were strong and earnest. She applied to a devout Franciscan friar for advice and comfort. She stated her convictions and told him of her long and fruitless seeking. After she had finished speaking to him, the friar remained silent for some time, in inward meditation and prayer. Then he said to her:

" Your efforts have been unsuccessful, because you have *sought without* what you can only *find within*. Accustom yourself to seek God in your heart, and you will not fail to find Him."

" When God has specially promised the thing,"

said Charles G. Finney, " we are bound to believe
we shall receive it when we pray for it. You have
no right to put in an ' if,' and say, ' Lord, *if* it be
Thy will, give me Thy Holy Spirit.' This is to in-
sult God. To put an ' if ' in God's promise when
God has put none there, is tantamount to charging
God with being insincere. It is like saying, ' O
God, if Thou art in earnest in making these promises, grant us the blessing we pray for.' "

We may fittingly conclude this chapter by quot-
ing a word of Adoniram Judson's, the noted missionary to Burma. Speaking of the prevailing
power of prayer he said:

" ' Nothing is impossible,' said one of the seven sages
of Greece, ' to industry.' Let us change the word, ' industry,' to ' persevering prayer,' and the motto will be
more Christian and more worthy of universal adoption.
God loves importunate prayer so much that He will not
give us much blessing without it. God says, ' Behold I
will do a new thing; now it shall spring forth; shall ye
not know it? I will even make a way in the wilderness
and rivers in the desert. This people have I formed for
myself; they shall shew forth my praise.' "